children's stories of the Bible from the old and new testaments

This book is presented

to   . . . .

from   . . . .

on   . . . .

This Deluxe Edition of Children's Stories of the Bible from the Old and New Testaments has been carefully checked for accuracy and has been approved by religious advisory consultants, comprising clergymen from the Protestant, Catholic and Jewish faiths.

children's stories of the Bible from the old and new testaments

edited by Barbara Taylor Bradford

illustrated by Laszlo Matulay

Old Testament stories by Merle Burnick

Playmore, Inc. New York, N.Y.

TABLE OF CONTENTS

the old testament

ADAM AND EVE

I n the beginning God created the heavens and the earth."
This is the first thing the Bible tells us. Out of the formless
darkness God made this beautiful world we live in. He made night and
day; He separated sky and earth, land and sea. And when the world was
formed, God created the living creatures on it.

Finally God made man and woman. The first man was called
Adam, a name meaning "man" or earth-man," for God had created man
out of the earth. The woman was named Eve, meaning "living."

Adam and Eve lived in a beautiful garden, where they had everything they needed, without worrying or working. This garden was
called Eden and they lived there in perfect happiness; and God talked
directly to them, telling them everything they needed to know. This
garden was also called Paradise.

God gave Adam one firm command: there was one tree whose fruit
he must not taste. This was the tree of the knowledge of good and evil.
Now Adam and Eve had never known anything bad, so they could not
understand the difference between good things and evil things. God
knew that if Adam and Eve learned that things could be bad, they and
all men and women after them would be subject to fears, anger, hatred

and sadness. Perfect happiness, such as theirs, would never again be known on earth.

One day, when Eve was admiring the beautiful fruit on the forbidden tree, she met a serpent, a creature we call a snake. The serpent urged her to pick the luscious fruit, but Eve knew that God had said she and Adam could have everything but this. The serpent, however, persuaded her that the fruit would make them as wise as God Himself. That, he explained, was the only reason God did not want them to eat it. Tempted by the serpent's words and the beauty of the fruit, Eve picked it, and both she and Adam tasted it.

Immediately they knew they had done wrong. Afraid and ashamed, they hid among the trees. God came into the garden that evening and, finding Adam and Eve hiding, made them tell Him what they had done. He sternly explained to them what they now faced.

They must leave the beautiful garden forever and go out into the world, where they must work long and hard to make the land produce enough to keep them alive. They would have children, but both they and their children would always know much hardship and sadness.

And God's words proved to be only too true.

No sooner had Adam and Eve's first two sons grown up than a terrible thing happened. Their sons were named Cain and Abel; Cain, the elder, was a farmer and Abel was a shepherd. Adam and Eve had not forgotten God, but since they could no longer talk with Him, each of the family offered gifts to God of the things they produced, to show that they knew they were still His children.

One day Cain and Abel fell into a bitter and violent quarrel, about which of their offerings was most pleasing to God. When it ended, Abel lay dead upon the ground, and the first deadful crime of man against man had been committed.

God punished Cain severely, but He did not kill him. He protected Cain from death at the hand of any man, and Cain lived to found a family of his own.

12

NOAH

For many hundreds of years after Adam and Eve were driven out of the Garden of Eden, the family of man multiplied and spread over the earth. Because Adam and Eve had disobeyed God and learned of evil things, the knowledge of wickedness was passed on, and as men learned more about the world, they learned more ways to be evil. Men forgot that they were the children of God and they grew more corrupt.

Finally God decided that man had grown so wicked He was sorry He had ever created human beings. And so God decided He would destroy all life on earth. There was one man, however, who remembered God and tried to live to please Him. His name was Noah. God spoke to Noah and told him the world had grown so violent that He was going to destroy the wicked, in a great flood that would cover the earth. But

God promised Noah that he and his family would be saved from the flood, and that one mother and one father of each living thing on the earth would be saved too.

God told Noah how to build an ark in which those to be saved would be protected from the waters of the flood. Noah followed God's instructions. And as the rains began and the waters of the sea rose over the land, Noah and his family and all the creatures were kept safe in the ark. The rains continued for forty days and the waters rose until the earth was a vast sea. Every living thing died in the terrible flood, except those sheltered in the ark.

For 150 days the earth was covered with water and then the flood began to recede from the land. After Noah had been in the ark nine months, the tops of the mountains appeared above the water. Forty days later Noah decided to find out if the water had lowered enough for them to leave the ark. He sent out a raven and a dove. The raven never returned. The dove, finding no place to set down, returned to the ark. Seven days later Noah sent the dove out again, and this time it returned with a branch of an olive tree. Noah then knew that at least part of the land was dry enough for plants to grow. After another seven days Noah sent out the dove once more, and this time it did not return. Noah knew then that the time had come to leave the ark.

As soon as Noah and the living creatures had left the ark, Noah built an altar where he gave thanks to God for being saved from the flood. God was pleased and made a promise to Noah that never again would He destroy living creatures as He had done with the great flood. The world was given again to man, for *his* use, as it had been given to Adam and Eve. God showed Noah the rainbow, that we see in the clouds after the rain. He told him that this would always be the sign of His promise.

ABRAHAM

fter the flood, Noah's three sons, Shem, Ham and Japeth, moved away and each went to live in a different place. They all had large families, and from their children and their children's children, and their descendants for many generations, the great nations of the ancient world came into being.

The stories in the Old Testament tell of one of these nations, a people who have been known as the Israelites, the Hebrews, and later the Jews. The Bible tells us of their beginnings, their growth as a nation, and the many troubles they faced; but most of all the Bible is concerned with the special relationship these people had with God. They have been called God's Chosen People because God made a solemn agreement with them. He promised to make them grow and prosper and to help them when they called upon Him. In return they must obey God's commands and keep alive the true knowledge of God, so that some day, through them, all mankind would know God.

This special relationship with God began with a man named Abram. He was a descendant of Noah's son, Shem. He and his wife Sarai lived in a place called Ur, in the land of the Chaldees on the

Euphrates River. They had no children, and Abram was already an old man when God spoke to him and told him he must move to a new land. There, God told Abram, he would have a family that would become a great nation and through his family all families would be blessed.

It took great faith to obey this command, but Abram kept this faith. Abram gathered his flocks of sheep and herds of cattle and set out with his wife, his very aged father Terah, a brother Nahor, and Lot, the son of another brother who had died.

They travelled up the Euphrates River to a place called Haran. There Terah died and Nahor decided to stay on. After his father's death, Abram continued his travels with Sarai and Lot. God had not told Abram where he was to settle, but when he came into a land called Canaan, God came to his tent and told Abram He was giving that land to his children and to their families forever. And this is the area which became the land of Israel, the home of the Hebrew people.

Abram and Lot raised sheep and cattle, so they had to move around a great deal to find the best grass for their animals. Shortly after they arrived in Canaan they went as far away as Egypt. There they were very successful, and when they returned to Canaan, they had so many cattle the land could hardly feed them. The herdsmen of Abram and those working for Lot began to quarrel about grazing rights, so Abram proposed they separate. He let Lot choose the land he wanted. Lot went down to the fertile plain of the River Jordan and Abram stayed in the mountains. As Lot prospered he moved into the city of Sodom.

Though he had chosen the richest land, Lot found nothing but trouble because he had settled among very evil people. First he was captured in a war and taken as a slave. When Abram heard of this he gathered together all the men who worked for him, over three hundred in all. He caught up with the conquering army, beat them in a surprise attack at night, and rescued Lot and all the other captives.

Abram brought Lot and the others back to Sodom, but refused to take any reward from the king of the city. And then he returned to his home in the mountains.

Abram was, by this time, a very old man. While he had many families living and working with him, he and his wife Sarai no longer expected to have any children of their own. God appeared again to Abram and told him more about the special relationship his family would have with God.

First, God changed Abram's name to Abraham, which means father of nations, and He changed Sarai's name to Sarah, which means princess. Then He told Abraham, as he was now called, that he and Sarah would have a son. Abraham was so astonished that he laughed. But God reassured him that the promises He had made to him would continue to his son, who would be called Isaac.

The next time the Lord returned to Abraham, He appeared as one of three travellers whom Abraham had invited to his tent to rest and

eat. This time Sarah heard that they were to have a son and she also laughed in astonishment, but was assured it would really happen.

Abraham walked down the road with the three travellers as they left. When they reached a point where they could look out toward Sodom, where Lot lived, God told Abraham that He was going to destroy the city along with the nearby city of Gomorrah, because the people living there had become so wicked. Abraham pleaded that it was not right to destroy the good people along with the bad, so God promised to spare the cities if He could find even ten good people living in them. He could not. The cities were destroyed in a great fire, but Lot was rescued by two angels who appeared at his house as travellers.

In those days Abraham, and others who loved God, showed this love by placing on an altar made of stones some of their best food, as a gift to God. Since they raised animals, this offering was usually a sheep or a calf.

God knew that He must impress upon Abraham that the promises He made were part of a solemn agreement. Abraham must obey all God's commands, no matter how terrible and painful they might seem. Only in this way could Abraham and his family understand the seriousness of the agreement they had entered into.

Therefore, God ordered Abraham to place his son Isaac upon an altar and kill him just as if he were a sheep. Abraham was shocked and filled with grief. He had promised to obey all commands of God, not just those that seemed right to him. He knew also that God had promised that Isaac would be the father of a great family which would lead to a great nation. Perhaps he thought God would somehow bring Isaac back to life. Whatever Abraham might have secretly hoped, this was surely the greatest test of faith a man could face.

Abraham set out to obey. He had three days to think over his decision and change his mind; three days while he travelled with his beloved son, to the mountain where God had said that he must sacrifice the boy.

When they started up the mountain Isaac spoke up and asked his father, "Where is the lamb for the offering?" Abraham replied, "My son, God will provide Himself a lamb."

Abraham built an altar, tied his son up, and laid him upon the altar. As he stood with the knife in his hand, a voice cried out, "Abraham! Abraham!" and he replied, "Here I am." And then an angel appeared and told him that God had seen that he had not withheld even his only son, whom he loved, from God. And so Isaac was spared.

Then God blessed Abraham and told him again of His great promise that Abraham's family would be a blessing to all people on earth.

JACOB

Isaac, the son of Abraham, married a woman named Rebekah who gave birth to twin boys named Esau and Jacob.

When the two boys grew up, Esau became his father's favorite because he loved the outdoors and was a skillful hunter like Isaac; and Jacob became his mother's favorite, because he was a quiet boy who preferred to stay at home and help her with her tasks.

Because they were so different from one another, Esau and Jacob had trouble getting along. One day Esau came in from the field very hungry. He saw Jacob boiling some soup and asked his brother to share it with him. Jacob refused to give Esau any soup, unless Esau sold his birthright to him. In those days a birthright was very important,

22

because it meant that the oldest son would inherit his father's land. Esau was older than Jacob and, therefore, was entitled to his father's land when Isaac died. Esau was so hungry, however, that he did not care about his birthright at that moment and agreed to sell it to Jacob for a bowl of soup.

As the years passed, Isaac grew old and blind. When he knew that he was ready to die he called Esau to his side to give him a final blessing. Before Isaac blessed Esau, he told his son to hunt a deer and prepare him a meal.

Rebekah was listening as Isaac spoke to Esau. When Esau had gone into the field to hunt, she prepared some meat and told Jacob to take it to his father, so that Isaac would bless Jacob instead of Esau. Jacob was reluctant to do this dishonest thing, but at last he agreed to follow his mother's wishes. He brought the meal to his father, and Isaac gave him his final blessing, thinking that Jacob was Esau.

As soon as Isaac had finished blessing Jacob and had sent him away, Esau returned with the meal he had prepared for his father. Then Isaac realized that he had been deceived and was deeply hurt and angered that Jacob could do such a thing.

From that day on Esau hated Jacob and vowed that he would kill him for taking away his birthright and his blessing. But the words of Esau were brought to Rebekah and she sent Jacob away to live with her brother, Laban, until Esau's anger cooled.

On the way to his uncle's house, Jacob stopped to rest for the night. While he was sleeping he dreamed that there was a ladder set up on earth. The top of the ladder reached heaven, and God's angels were climbing up and down. At the very top of the ladder, God stood above all and said to Jacob, "I am the Lord, the God of Abraham and Isaac. The land on which you lie I will give to you and your descendants; and your descendants shall spread like dust to the west and to the east, to the north and to the south."

The following morning Jacob arose and took the stone which he had used to sleep on and set it up as a pillar. Then he poured oil upon it, to mark it as a spot of blessed memory. And he called the place where God had visited him Bethel, which means the house of God.

Jacob continued on his journey until he came to a field where Laban's beautiful daughter Rachel was tending the sheep. Rachel greeted Jacob warmly and brought him to see her father.

Jacob worked for Laban for a month, and during this time he grew to love Rachel. When Laban asked him what his wages should be, Jacob replied that he would like to have Rachel in marriage and agreed to work seven years for her hand.

At the end of seven years, Laban prepared a marriage feast, but in the place of Rachel, Laban substituted his older daughter Leah, who was not Jacob's favorite. Leah wore a veil so that no one could see her face. At the end of the marriage ceremony Leah was Jacob's wife. Laban had tricked Jacob, just as Jacob had once deceived his brother and his father.

Laban explained that it was the custom of the land for the oldest daughter to be married first. He promised Jacob that in return for serving him for another seven years, he would also receive Rachel for a wife.

At the end of seven years Rachel became Jacob's wife, but Laban continued to treat Jacob badly and often refused to pay him the wages he had promised. Finally, Jacob could not bear this treatment any longer. He gathered his wives and children on camels and set out for Canaan, the land of his birth.

Before Jacob arrived in Canaan, he sent messengers to tell his brother Esau that he was truly sorry he had cheated him, that he was coming in peace. Jacob's messenger, however, brought back bad news. Esau was coming with four hundred men to fight Jacob and his people.

That same night, Jacob was bothered by his conscience and went off by himself to think about his past actions. While he was alone a man came and wrestled with him until the break of day. Then Jacob learned that the man with whom he had fought was an angel of God, who said to him, "Because you have accepted the challenge to fight and have not given up, you have earned God's favor." Then the angel changed Jacob's name to Israel, a name that means "He who struggles with God" or "The Reliable One."

When the angel had left, Jacob looked into the distance and saw Esau coming with his four hundred men. As Esau approached Jacob bowed himself to the ground seven times. And instead of fighting, Esau ran to meet Jacob and embraced him and wept because he was so glad to see his brother. Jacob was likewise filled with joy because he had found favor in his brother's eyes. Both men returned to Canaan with their families, and, as God had foretold, Jacob's descendants spread over the face of the earth.

JOSEPH

acob, the son of Isaac, had twelve sons. They did not all have
the same mother, because Jacob had been married more than
once. Jacob raised sheep, and his sons, who worked as shepherds, were
strong and often violent men, except for Joseph, the son of Rachel. He
was a dreamy, thoughtful boy and his rough older brothers did not like
him.

To make their resentment worse, Joseph was his father's favorite
son and was treated better than the other brothers. When Joseph was

about seventeen, his father gave him a long robe with sleeves. Shepherds dress in very rough clothes, even today, and this long colorful robe was a ceremonial garment. The robe made Joseph's brothers even more jealous than before.

To make matters still worse, Joseph told the family of two dreams he had had. In one of the dreams, the brothers were working in the field binding grain into sheaves. (Sheaves are bundles that are stood on end in the field, so that they can be collected later.) In his dream, Joseph saw the sheaves that his brothers had tied, bow down before his sheaf. His second dream angered even his father. He dreamed that the sun and moon and eleven stars bowed down to him. Jacob asked Joseph angrily, "Shall I and thy mother and thy brethren indeed come to bow down ourselves to thee to the earth?"

One day Jacob sent Joseph with a message for his brothers, who were tending their sheep far out in the fields. The sight of the long, rich robe was more than the brothers could bear. As he approached, they plotted together to kill Joseph and throw his body in a pit. His oldest brother Reuben could not bring himself to commit this terrible crime, so he suggested they should not kill him, but simply throw Joseph in the pit. Reuben thought that he would return to rescue the boy later. When they had torn off Joseph's beautiful robe, however, and thrown him into the pit, they saw some merchants coming down the road. The other brothers decided they would sell Joseph to the merchants as a slave. In those days many poor families sent some of their children to work for wealthy men, since they could not always take care of all their children.

The brothers then realized that they would have to answer to their father for Joseph's disappearance. So they killed a young goat and dipped Joseph's robe in the blood and took it to Jacob. The father was sure that his favorite son had been killed by wild animals and he could not be comforted, in his grief.

The merchants took Joseph with them into Egypt, and there they sold him to Potiphar, an important officer of the Pharaoh, the king of

Egypt. Joseph was a faithful and valuable servant, and Potiphar put him in charge of his household. After a time Potiphar's wife made trouble for Joseph and he was thrown into prison.

But God continued to watch over Joseph, giving him the power to know the meanings of dreams. Also in prison with him were Pharaoh's butler and baker, who had offended the king. One night they both had dreams, which they told to Joseph. The butler dreamed that there were three branches with buds on them. The buds turned to blossoms, and the blossoms ripened into grapes. The butler dreamed that he pressed the grapes into Pharaoh's cup and placed the cup in Pharaoh's hand. Joseph told the butler that his dream meant that within three days the Pharaoh would free him from prison. He would get his job back and

hand Pharaoh his cup, as he did before when he was Pharaoh's butler.

The baker dreamed that there were three cake baskets on his head. In the top basket there were all kinds of baked food for Pharaoh, but birds were eating out of his basket. Joseph told the baker that *his* dream meant that in three days the Pharaoh would hang him, from a tree full of birds.

At the end of three days the Pharaoh had a birthday. He made a feast for all his servants. He freed the butler from prison and gave him back his job, but he hanged the baker.

Before the butler left prison, Joseph asked him to help get him out of prison once he was back in the Pharaoh's service. But the man forgot about Joseph for two years.

Then one day, the Pharaoh told his servant about a strange dream of his own and asked the butler if he knew anyone who could interpret it. The butler remembered Joseph, who was still in prison. He told Pharaoh how Joseph had interpreted his dream and the baker's dream, and the Pharaoh immediately sent for Joseph.

Pharaoh told Joseph he had dreamed that seven fat cattle were grazing in a field, and seven lean cattle came up and ate the fat cattle. Then there were seven good ears of corn on a stalk, and seven withered ears grew up and ate the good ears.

Joseph told the Pharaoh that God was telling him, through the dream, that there would be seven years of rich harvests; but in the seven years that followed not enough rain would fall and not enough food would be grown. Joseph advised the Pharaoh to appoint someone to buy up all the spare food he could obtain, during the seven good years.

Pharaoh was deeply impressed with Joseph, so he appointed the young man to handle this very important job for him. When the famine came seven years later, Egypt was the only land that had food. The surrounding countries had to send to Egypt to buy food. They had to deal with Joseph, who was now second in importance only to the Pharaoh.

The famine had also struck Canaan, the land where Joseph's family still lived, and Jacob had to send his sons to Egypt to buy grain. He kept his youngest son Benjamin with him.

When the brothers appeared before Joseph, they did not recognize him, but he knew them at once. Joseph spoke harshly to his brothers. He accused them of being spies and put them in jail. He noticed that Benjamin was not with them and he wanted to see him. This was Joseph's only full brother; the others had different mothers and were, therefore, his half-brothers.

Later Joseph gave his brothers a generous supply of grain, but demanded that one of them be kept in prison, until the others returned with Benjamin. The brothers were very unhappy about this and talked among themselves. They decided that this must be punishment, for the way they had treated their brother Joseph years before. Hearing this Joseph wept, but he did not let his brothers see him weep. He still treated them harshly and tied up his brother Simeon. And he put him in prison, where he would stay until the others returned with Benjamin.

When the brothers went back to Canaan, they pleaded with Jacob to let Benjamin go with them to Egypt. They promised to protect Benjamin with their lives. Simeon was still a prisoner in Egypt; the famine was still in the land of Canaan; and Jacob's family needed food, so he sadly consented to let his sons take Benjamin with them.

When Joseph saw Benjamin, he was so moved that again he left the room and wept. When Joseph returned to the room and faced his brothers, he was still harsh and wanted to test them further. In the morning, Joseph instructed his servants to fill the brothers' bags with grain and to put his silver cup into Benjamin's bag. Then Joseph demanded that the one who had the cup be kept as his slave. His officers searched every bag and when they came to Benjamin, they found the silver cup.

The brothers refused to part with Benjamin. They told Joseph that their father was an old man and would be in deep sorrow if he lost his beloved son, for he had already lost another son, who was torn to pieces by a wild animal.

Then Judah, one of the brothers, pleaded to let Benjamin go back with them and even offered himself as a slave instead. Moved by this display of brotherly love, Joseph broke down and told them, "I am your brother, Joseph, whom you sold into Egypt." And he and his brothers wept for joy to see each other again.

Joseph then sent for his father, who could not believe his good fortune until he actually saw Joseph. Jacob brought his family to live in Egypt, and they stayed there for many years because they were well treated by the Pharaoh, who admired Joseph so much.

MOSES

The Pharaoh of Egypt who had been so kind to Joseph's family died after many years, and a cruel king took his place. When this king saw how the Israelites grew and prospered in his land, he placed them in slavery and set over them harsh task-masters, to watch them while they worked. But even this act did not crush the spirit of the Israelites or Hebrews, as they were called. They continued to prosper and raise healthy families. The Pharaoh of Egypt was so angry at this, he issued an order demanding the death of every male child born to a Hebrew mother.

At this time in Egypt a Hebrew woman gave birth to a healthy son. For three months she ignored the Pharaoh's order and hid the baby safely in her home. When she could hide him no longer, she made a basket out of bulrushes and covered it with pitch to make it float; then she put her son in it and placed the basket among the reeds along the river bank. She left her daughter to wait and see what would happen to the child.

After a short time the Pharaoh's daughter, attended by her servants, came down to the river to bathe. As she came near the river, she saw the basket among the reeds and asked her servants to bring it to her. When she opened the basket and saw the baby crying, Pharaoh's daughter took pity on him and told her maidens that she wanted to raise the child as her own. Hearing this, the baby's sister, who was hiding in the reeds, went to Pharaoh's daughter and told her that she knew a Hebrew woman who had lost her own son. She said the woman could nurse the child. Pharaoh's daughter told the girl to bring the woman to her.

The Hebrew girl went home and brought back the baby's own mother, who took the baby and nursed him for a few months. Then the woman returned him to Pharaoh's daughter, who raised him as her own son and called him Moses, which means "drawn out of the water."

One day, when Moses was a young man, he went among the Hebrew slaves and saw an Egyptian officer beating one of them. He became so angry that he rushed upon the Egyptian and killed him. Moses knew that the Pharaoh would punish him for his actions, so he fled to the land of Midian and remained there for many years as a shepherd.

One day, while Moses was leading his sheep into the wilderness to graze, he came to Horeb, the mountain of God. God appeared to Moses in a flame of fire from the midst of a bush. When Moses looked carefully, he saw that the fire continued and yet the bush was not burnt at all. This marvelous act was God's way of calling Moses, for He had something very important to tell him.

God told Moses that He had seen the suffering and sadness of the
Israelite slaves in Egypt and that He wanted Moses to lead the people
out of bondage. He also promised that He would help Moses lead the
Israelites into a land flowing with milk and honey.

Moses did not understand how he could lead the Israelites to freedom, but God assured him that He would be with him, enabling him
to perform wonders that would make the Pharaoh tremble.

So Moses and his brother Aaron went to Egypt and said to the
Pharaoh, "The Lord, the God of Israel says, 'Let my people go.'"
Pharaoh replied, "Who is the Lord that I should heed His voice and let
Israel go?" Then Moses performed a miracle to show the power of God.
At God's command, Aaron cast his rod down before Pharaoh, and to the
amazement of everyone the rod turned into a snake. But the Pharaoh
was unmoved and unimpressed, and he refused to let the people of
Israel go.

At God's command, Moses and Aaron went to the Pharaoh the next morning while he was walking by the River Nile and asked him again to let the Israelites go. When Pharaoh refused, Aaron struck the water with his rod and turned the Nile into blood, so that neither man nor beast could drink from it. Still Pharaoh would not heed God's wrath and refused to let the people of Israel go. Instead he gave the slaves heavier work and treated them harshly.

To punish the Egyptians for their wickedness, God sent to Egypt nine more horrible plagues. He overran the land with frogs and locusts; He caused darkness over the land; and each plague was worse than the other. The Pharaoh became so frightened, he promised Moses that he would let the people go, but as soon as God removed the plague from the land, the Pharaoh would take back his word and keep the Israelites in bondage.

Then God sent one final affliction. The Angel of Death came to each house in Egypt and killed the first-born child of each Egyptian family. But the angel passed over the homes of the Hebrews, who had marked their doors with a sign, just as Moses had told them to do. This was the beginning of the Passover, which is still celebrated all over the world by Hebrew people.

Pharaoh's child was also taken by the Angel of Death, and in despair Pharaoh finally told Moses to take his people and leave Egypt forever.

So the Israelites gathered their possessions and left, before the Pharaoh could change his mind again. God commanded Moses to lead the people toward the Red Sea. When Pharaoh realized that the Israelites were actually gone from Egypt, he was angry at himself for letting them escape. So he set out with his entire army and chariots, to overtake them and bring them back to slavery.

When the Israelites saw Pharaoh's army coming after them, they panicked and turned against Moses. They told him that they would rather serve in bondage than die in the wilderness, but Moses told them not to be afraid, that God would watch out for their safety.

Then God created a great cloud which He placed between the Israelites and the Egyptians, so that Pharaoh and his army could not get to Moses and his people that night. He also commanded Moses to stretch out his hand over the Red Sea, and as he did so, the Lord drove the sea back by a strong east wind. The Red Sea divided and left a dry path for the Israelites to cross. Moses and his people hurried to the other side with Pharaoh's army following close behind. As soon as the last Israelite had crossed, God commanded Moses to stretch out his hand again over the Red Sea. When he did this, the waters of the Red Sea went back into place and swallowed up the Egyptians, who were in the midst of crossing. Not one escaped.

Then Moses and his people set out into the wilderness. After several days, the people again turned against their leader, this time because they were hungry. They told Moses that they would rather be back in bondage in Egypt, where at least they would have food.

That evening God told Moses that He had heard the complaints of the Israelites and that by morning He would give them food. When they awoke, they saw quail all over their camp, and thin flakes of meal that covered the ground like frost. Moses said to them, "It is the bread which the Lord has given you to eat." Then the Israelites gathered the fine flakes of bread and called their new food "manna."

As the Israelites moved further into the wilderness, the people of Amalek attacked them; and Moses chose a man named Joshua to lead his people in battle. Then Moses went on top of a hill with the rod of God in his hand. Whenever he held up his hands, Israel gained in the battle; but whenever he lowered his hands, the Israelites lost ground. Finally Moses' hands grew so tired that Aaron and another man named Hur had to hold them up for him. The two men remained by Moses' side until sundown, when Israel had defeated Amalek.

Soon after this Moses and his people traveled to the wilderness of Sinai and camped below a mountain. At Sinai, God called to Moses and told him that in three days He would come down upon Mount Sinai for all the people of Israel to see. On the morning of the third day there was thunder and lightning. Then a great heavy cloud came over Mount Sinai, and Moses brought his people out of the camp to see God. Moses spoke, and God answered with fire and thunder.

Then Moses left his people and went by himself to the top of Mount Sinai. Here Moses received the Ten Commandments—two tablets of stone on which were written the laws that God had set for the people of Israel.

Moses spent forty days on Mount Sinai, listening to the words of God. The people of Israel thought that Moses would never come down, and began to lose faith in God. They asked Aaron to build them an idol to worship. Aaron did not want to build the idol, but the people came to him every day, and finally he agreed to satisfy their request. He asked the people for their gold earrings and other jewelry which he melted down and shaped into a golden calf.

When Moses came down from Mount Sinai with the stone tablets in his hands, he heard a great noise. Looking at the foot of the mountain, he saw the Israelites dancing and singing around the golden calf. Moses was so angry that he threw down the tablets of stone and broke them. He took the golden calf, set it on the fire, and crushed it to dust. Then he scattered it on the water and made the people of Israel drink it. Moses asked Aaron how he could let the people sin like this, and Aaron could not answer. Moses called for those who were on the Lord's side to come forward and he commanded them to slay all those who still wanted to worship idols.

Moses returned to Mount Sinai to talk to God and ask His forgiveness for the sins of the people. At length God relented and restored to the people of Israel the Ten Commandments:

I am the Lord your God. You shall have no other gods before me.

You shall not worship any graven image.

You shall not take the name of the Lord your God in vain.

Remember to keep holy the sabbath day.

Honor your father and your mother.

You shall not kill.

You shall not commit adultery.

You shall not steal.

You shall not bear false witness against your neighbor.

You shall not covet anything that is your neighbor's.

God kept Moses and the Israelites in the wilderness for forty years, making them tough and strong, and welding them into a nation. When Moses was ready to die, God sent him to the top of a mountain which overlooked the valley of the Jordan River at Jericho. And He told him that that rich, fertile country was the land of milk and honey that He had promised the Israelites. God told Moses that he himself would never enter this land, but the children of Israel would.

Soon after God had shown Moses the Promised Land, Moses died at the age of one hundred and twenty. All of Israel mourned the loss of their great leader, who had brought them out of slavery through the wilderness, and made them a united people, thereby showing them how God protects and guides His children.

JOSHUA

Before Moses died he chose a man named Joshua to succeed him, as leader of the Israelites.

At God's command Joshua told his people to prepare their provisions, for in three days they would cross the Jordan River into the Promised Land.

In the evening, Joshua sent two men secretly to look at the land, especially the city of Jericho. The two men went to the house of a woman named Rahab. When the king of Jericho found out that two men of Israel had come to search his land, he went to Rahab's house and demanded to see the men. But the woman had taken Joshua's messengers to the roof and had hidden them under stalks of flax. She told the king that the men of Israel had gone away toward the Jordan River.

When the king and his men left her home, Rahab went up to the roof and spoke to the two men of Israel. She told them that the people of Jericho were afraid, because they knew that God had given the land to the Israelites. Joshua's messengers promised to repay Rahab's kindness, by protecting her family when the Israelites came to take the land.

Then the woman took a rope and helped the men climb down the wall of Jericho. The men told Rahab to keep her family inside the house during the battle and to put a scarlet thread in her window. If she did this, no man of Israel would touch her house.

The two men went back and told Joshua about the fear in Jericho and about the woman who had protected them in her home. Joshua saw that the time was right to move his people into the Promised Land.

At the end of three days, Joshua commanded his priests to take the Ark of the Covenant, which contained the Laws of God, and to carry it to the Jordan River. As soon as the priests' feet touched the waters of the Jordan, God caused the river to stop flowing. All the people of Israel crossed the dry river bed, and when the last of the Israelites had crossed the Jordan, the priests came across. As soon as they lifted their feet from the river bed, God caused the waters of the Jordan to flow again.

Joshua had his people camp outside of the city of Jericho, which was protected on all sides by a great wall. At God's command, Joshua had his people march around the wall of the city for six days. The priests carried the Ark of the Covenant and they also blew trumpets made of rams' horns. The only sound that was heard came from the trumpets, for Joshua had commanded his people to be absolutely silent.

On the seventh day, Joshua had the Israelites march around the city seven times. On the seventh time around, when the priests had blown the trumpets, Joshua said to his people, "Shout; for the Lord has given you the city." The people all shouted together, and the great wall around the city of Jericho crumbled and fell.

And so the people of Israel went in and took the city, but they did not harm the house with the scarlet cord in the window, because they knew it belonged to Rahab, who had sheltered the messengers.

Joshua ordered his men to collect all the gold and silver treasures of the city and put them in the Temple, as a dedication to God. One man, named Achan, stole a bar of gold, some silver, and a beautiful mantle and hid them in his tent. This was in direct violation of the Laws of God and brought great trouble upon all of Israel. Because of the greed of one man, many suffered. When he was caught, he confessed, and because he had sinned against the Lord and had brought His wrath upon the people, he and his family were killed. And a great heap of stones was piled on top of them.

It was then that Joshua led his army once more against the neighboring city of Ai, whose inhabitants threatened to destroy the people of Israel. Joshua brought half of his army into a valley below the city of Ai. He secretly placed the other half of his army above the city. When the king of Ai saw Joshua's army in the valley beneath, he led all of his people down into the valley to fight the Israelites. In the meantime, the other

half of Joshua's army came out of hiding from above, entered the empty city of Ai, and set fire to it. The people of Ai, caught between the two armies, had no place to which to retreat, and they were all captured by the Israelites.

Joshua spent the rest of his life dividing the Promised Land among the people of Israel and helping them to overcome their enemies. Finally, all of the land which God had promised to them belonged to the Israelites. Joshua reminded the people again that if they did not obey God's Commandments, and if they worshipped idols, they would lose the Promised Land.

45

GIDEON

The people of Israel sinned in the eyes of God. They did not follow His commandments, and they worshipped idols. So God made the people of Israel suffer under the rule of cruel Midianites. The Midianites forced the people of Israel to live in dens and caves in the mountains. When the Israelites tried to farm the land, the Midianites would attack them, destroy their camps, their sheep and their crops. For seven years the Israelites suffered under these harsh rulers.

God saw how sad the people of Israel were and decided that they had been punished long enough. He chose a man named Gideon to lead them to victory. Gideon was at his wine press when God visited him, and when God told him what he was to do, Gideon asked, "How can I deliver Israel when my people are the weakest in the country?" God reassured Gideon and said, "I will be with you, and you shall smite all of the Midianites as if they were one man."

Gideon wanted proof that this was really God who was speaking to him. So Gideon prepared a lamb, unleavened bread, and broth as a sacrifice. Then he asked God to give a sign of His presence. God told Gideon to pour the broth over the lamb and the unleavened bread. Then God reached out with the tip of His staff and touched the meat and bread. Instantly they burst into flame. And Gideon knew that this was indeed God speaking to him.

That night God visited Gideon again and told him to tear down the altar of Baal, an idol which the people of Israel were worshipping. In its place, Gideon was to build an altar to God.

When the men of the town arose early in the morning, they saw that the altar of Baal was broken. When they found out that Gideon had destroyed the altar, they wanted to kill him. But Gideon's father, Joash, told them if Baal was really a god, then he should punish Gideon himself. Gideon's life was spared.

Gideon began to think about the enormous task of leading the Israelites against the Midianites. Once again he turned to God for comfort. Gideon said to God, "If you will give Israel victory with my help as you said, behold, I am laying a sheepskin on the ground. If the sheepskin is wet in the morning and the ground is dry, then I will know that you will help Israel to victory."

Early the next morning Gideon arose and saw that the ground was dry. Then he felt the sheepskin, and it was wet; he squeezed a bowl of water from it.

Gideon, reassured by the power of God, gathered his men to fight the Midianites. God looked at Gideon's men and told him that there were too many of them. God told Gideon to tell all the people who were afraid to fight, to go back to their homes. Gideon tested his army; twenty-two thousand returned, and ten thousand remained.

God saw the ten thousand men, and he told Gideon that there were still too many men. God asked Gideon to watch his army when they were drinking water from a stream. Gideon was to put the men who lapped the water with their tongues in one group; the men who drank the water from their hands were to be in another group. Three hundred men drank water from their hands, and God chose these men to help Gideon.

Gideon gave each of these three hundred men a trumpet and a jar with a torch inside it. He told his men to follow him. "When I blow the trumpet, you blow your trumpets." The men reached the Midianite camp at night. Gideon gave the signal, and the three hundred men blew their trumpets and smashed their jars so that the torches would light up the darkness. The men of the Midianite army were so surprised by the noise, the confusion, and the sudden attack that they fled to another town for safety.

Gideon and his men captured the two Midianite princes, Oreb and Zeeb, and had them put to death. Then they went in search of the two Midianite kings, Zebah and Zalmunna.

Gideon's men were tired and hungry from fighting during the night, so they stopped at the camp of Succoth and asked for bread. But the kings of Succoth cared only for their own safety. They were afraid that the Midianites would win the battle and then turn on the people of Succoth for giving bread to Gideon's men. So the kings refused to help Gideon's army.

When Gideon saw that the people of Succoth had faith in nothing, that they lived in fear of their fellow men, Gideon's faith in God was strengthened. He led his men to the city of Karkor where the Midianite kings and their army were staying. He entered the city by a road that was little used and surprised the Midianite army once again. He captured the army and the two Midianite kings, Zebah and Zalmunna.

Gideon asked his people to give him all the earrings they had taken from the Midianites. Then he melted the golden earrings and made a statue to symbolize the victory of the Israelites.

Once again, the people of Israel were free to live in peace and worship God. The people were so happy and grateful to Gideon that they wanted to make him their king. But Gideon refused and said to his people, "I will not rule over you, and my son will not rule over you; God will rule over you."

And there was peace in Israel for forty years.

RUTH

The Old Testament tells us that there was once a shortage of food, in the city of Bethlehem. To escape the famine, one man named Elimelech took his wife Naomi and his two sons Mahlon and Chilion to the nearby land of Moab. Elimelech died there and ten years later Mahlon and Chilion died too, leaving Naomi without a husband, sons or grandchildren.

Naomi felt very much alone and became homesick for her own people in Bethlehem. When she heard that God had given the city food, she decided to return. The widows of Mahlon and Chilion, who were named Ruth and Orpah, wanted to go with her, but Naomi told them to stay in Moab where they could marry again and have children. The trip back to Bethlehem would be long and hard, and they would be leaving their homes and families to live among strangers.

Orpah agreed to remain in Moab with her family, and she kissed Naomi good-bye, but Ruth stayed close to Naomi's side and said, "Where

you go I will go, and where you lodge I will lodge; your people shall be my people, and your God my God."

Naomi knew that she had a faithful companion in Ruth. Together the two women made the journey to Bethlehem. When they arrived, the people there were very surprised to see Naomi after so long a time, and the women of the city said to her, "Can this be Naomi?" She answered, "Don't call me Naomi" (a name which means "pleasant"); "Call me Mara" (which is the Hebrew word for "bitter"). "God has dealt very bitterly with me. I went away with a husband and sons, and now they are gone."

Ruth understood Naomi's sadness, but she also knew that they had to make the best of things. It happened that it was the harvest season in Bethlehem, so Ruth said to Naomi, "Let me go to the field and glean among the ears of grain." Gleaning means gathering whatever is left on the ground after the harvest. In those days the poor people were allowed to follow the reapers and keep the grain that they found.

Ruth went to glean and happened to reach a part of the field that belonged to a man named Boaz, who was a relative of Naomi's late husband Elimelech. Boaz saw Ruth and asked his servant who she was. The servant said, "She is the Moabite maiden who came back with Naomi from the country of Moab, and she has been gleaning from early morning until now, without resting for a moment." Boaz was so impressed by Ruth's devotion to Naomi and her courage in moving to a strange land, that he told Ruth to stay in his field where she would be protected and would find plenty of food.

According to ancient Hebrew custom, a woman who lost her husband had the right to marry her husband's next of kin. Naomi wished to see her daughter-in-law married again and provided for, so she suggested that Ruth ask Boaz to marry her. Because Ruth was a good woman Boaz consented to marry and take care of her. They were blessed with a son to carry on the family name and inherit the land, and this son was to become the grandfather of King David.

SAMUEL

An Israelite woman named Hannah was very sad because she was childless. So she told her husband Elkanah that she was going to the Temple of God to pray for a son.

In her prayers Hannah promised that if she had a son she would give him to God for a servant. God saw how much Hannah wanted a child, and after some months had passed He blessed her with a son, whom she called Samuel.

Samuel remained with his mother for a little while. Then she brought him to the House of God, where he lived with a priest named Eli and his two sons, Hophni and Phinehas. Here Samuel learned how to serve God as a priest.

As Samuel grew older, he grew in God's favor because he was devoted and faithful. He was also loved by the people of Israel, because he performed his priestly duties well. Hophni and Phinehas, on the other hand, became more and more disliked because they deceived God and cheated the people. One of the duties of the priests was to go from house to house and collect a portion of meat from each family, to be used as an offering to God. Hophni and Phinehas were so greedy, they demanded more meat than the people could afford to give. They then kept the best parts of the meat for themselves and gave the remainder to God.

One night Samuel was in bed and God called to him. He told Samuel that He was going to destroy Eli's family because of the sins of Hophni and Phinehas. He would raise a faithful prophet to serve Him. God also spoke to Eli and warned him that he and his sons would die on the same day.

Some years passed, and Israel went into battle with the Philistine invaders. The people of Israel asked Eli to bring the Ark of the Covenant onto the battlefield. In the fighting that day, the Philistines defeated the Israelites, killed Eli's sons, and took the Holy Ark. Eli was a very old man at the time, and when he heard the news, he died from the shock. Thus Eli's family was destroyed, as God had told Samuel it would be. God then raised Samuel as the beloved prophet of all Israel.

The Ark of God was in the country of the Philistines for seven months. During this time, God afflicted the Philistines with a terrible plague. The Philistines were so frightened that they returned the Ark to the Israelites, along with five golden mice, which they had molded in the image of the mice that had carried the plague.

Samuel gathered all his people together and asked them to pray to God for strength against the Philistines. That night, as the Israelites prepared to attack, God thundered with a mighty voice, that frightened and confused the Philistines. Then the Israelites entered the Philistine city and captured it.

Samuel took a large stone and marked the place where God had helped the Israelites subdue their enemy. Then there was peace in the land, and Samuel continued to serve the Israelites as their prophet for as long as he lived.

SAUL

hen Samuel the prophet became old, he made his sons judges over Israel, but they were not good men like their father. They were greedy men, who used their power to destroy justice and hurt people. Finally, the leaders of the city, knowing that the other nations were ruled by kings, gathered together and asked Samuel to find them a king to rule the land.

Samuel went before God and asked for help in choosing a leader. God told Samuel, "Tomorrow I will send to you a man from the land of Benjamin, and you shall annoint him to be king over my people Israel."

The next morning a handsome young man named Saul came to Samuel's city, looking for some lost donkeys. Saul's servant suggested that he visit Samuel, the wise prophet, and ask him where he should look for the animals. When Samuel met Saul, God told him, "Here is the man of whom I spoke to you! It is he who shall rule over my people." Samuel invited Saul and his servant to dinner and made a big feast for them. He gave Saul a place at the head of the table and told him not to worry about his donkeys, for they had been found.

After dinner, Samuel revealed God's word to Saul. Saul could not believe that he had been chosen for such an important job, because he came from a very poor, humble family. Samuel assured Saul that God looked into the hearts of men and did not choose them for their riches. Then Samuel took a vial of oil and poured it on Saul's head as a symbol of God's blessing, and proclaimed him king over Israel.

The next day Samuel gathered the people of Israel together, to show them their new king. When Saul stood before the people, he was a full head taller than everyone else. There was no one like him in the land, and all the people shouted to him, "Long live the king!"

In the midst of their happy celebration, Samuel spoke seriously to the people and reminded them that if they or their new king did evil in the eyes of God or failed to serve God in truth, they would all be punished severely.

Saul ruled during a time when Israel was at war with neighboring tribes. One of these tribes was the Amalekites. At God's command, Samuel told Saul to lead the Israelites in battle against the Amalekites and not to spare one living thing, be it man, woman, infant, ox, sheep, camel, or donkey. So Saul gathered a large army from all the tribes of Israel and defeated the Amalekites, destroying the people, but sparing the Amalekite king and also the best sheep, the best oxen, and the best lambs.

After the defeat of the Amalekites, God said to Samuel, "I repent that I have made Saul king, for he has turned back from following me, and has not performed my commandments." Hearing this, Samuel became very angry and went to see Saul. When Samuel heard the bleating of the sheep and the lowing of the oxen, he asked Saul why he had disobeyed God by sparing the best animals. Saul replied that he intended to use the best animals as sacrifices to God.

Then Samuel spoke harshly to Saul and told him that God believed that Saul had saved the best animals for his own personal gain. Samuel reminded Saul that his first duty was to obey God's commandments, not to make sacrifices. "Fear the Lord and serve him faithfully," Samuel had told Saul and all the people of Israel. "If you do wickedly you shall be swept away."

Because Saul had disobeyed God, he was not worthy to be king.

DAVID

God was not pleased with the way Saul was leading the Israelites. He told Samuel, the prophet, that He was going to choose a new leader from among the sons of Jesse the Bethlehemite.

Samuel sent for Jesse and his sons, but when the men stood before him, Samuel received no sign from God that any of these men were chosen to be king. Samuel said to Jesse, "Are all your sons here?" And Jesse replied, "They are all here but the youngest, who is at home tending the sheep."

At Samuel's request, Jesse sent for his son immediately. The boy's name was David. He was very handsome, with red cheeks and beautiful eyes. And God said to Samuel, "Arise, anoint him; for this is he." Then Samuel took a horn of oil and anointed David in the presence of his brothers and father. From that day on, God blessed David and made him strong.

King Saul knew that he had lost the favor of God, and often he was bothered by evil thoughts. One day, when Saul was very unhappy, he asked his servant to find a man who could entertain him by playing the lyre, which is an ancient instrument that resembles a small harp.

Saul's servant told him about David, the son of Jesse, who was very skillful at playing the lyre. Saul sent his messenger to Jesse and said, "Send David your son to me."

Jesse sent David with bread, a skin of wine, and a kid to give to Saul. Then David played the lyre, and Saul's evil thoughts disappeared. David found favor in Saul's eyes and agreed to remain in Saul's service.

The Israelites were still troubled by the Philistines. The champion of the Philistines was a giant named Goliath. Goliath towered over the rest of the people. He wore a bronze helment, a heavy coat of armor, and steel coverings for his legs. He carried an enormous spear. Goliath said to the

Israelites, "Choose a man for yourselves, and let him come down to me. If he is able to fight with me and kill me, then we will be your servants."

Every day David visited his father's house in order to feed the sheep. Three of David's brothers had joined Saul in battle against the Philistines, and one day David's father asked him to bring some bread and cheese to them.

David took the food and greeted his brothers on the battlefield. As he stood talking to them, Goliath the giant came out of the Philistine camp and repeated his words, as he had been doing for forty days. No man in all of Israel would come to fight the giant. The people were so afraid when they saw Goliath, that they fled from him.

When David observed how the giant held the Israelites in fear, he was very moved and his courage grew. David visited Saul and said to the king, "Let no man's heart fail because of him, I will go and fight with this Philistine." And Saul said to David, "You cannot fight with this Philistine, for you are a young boy and he is a man of war." But David told Saul that he was not afraid. When he was a shepherd, he had fought wild bears and lions who attacked his lambs. David said he would treat Goliath just like a beast of prey.

Saul agreed to let David fight the giant. He clothed him with armor and a bronze helmet and put a sword over his shoulder. But David was not used to armor. He could not move because the armor was too heavy for him. So he took off the helmet, the armor and the sword, and in their place he chose a slingshot and five smooth stones from the brook. Then he went to the Philistine camp.

When Goliath saw David, he thought that the boy was mocking him, because David was so young and came without armor and the usual weapons. He said to David, "Come to me, and I will give your flesh to the birds of the air and the beasts of the field." And David replied, "You come to me with a sword and a spear for protection, but I come to you with the God of the armies of Israel for protection. God will deliver you into my hand, and I will strike you down."

Then Goliath came near to meet David, and David put his hand in his bag and took out a stone which he placed in his slingshot. He shot Goliath on the forehead, and the giant fell on his face to the ground. Then David took Goliath's sword and killed him.

When the Philistines saw that their champion was dead, they fled, and the Israelites chased them from the land. Saul spoke to David and asked him to remain in his service forever. David agreed.

As time passed, Saul grew jealous of David because David was superior to him in battle and had won the hearts of the people. Saul feared that David would soon take his kingdom away from him. Twice while David was playing the lyre for Saul, Saul cast his spear at him. But David jumped out of the way.

Then Saul spoke to his son, Jonathan, and asked for his help in getting rid of David. But Jonathan loved David and admired him for his courage and good deeds. Instead of killing David as his father had instructed, Jonathan helped David to escape from Saul's kingdom.

When Saul found out that David had escaped alive, he was furious. Saul set out with his men to find David in the wilderness, for he had heard that David and his men had settled in a place called Engedi. After he had searched Engedi for a while, Saul became tired and entered a cave to rest, not knowing that further in the cave, David and his men were also resting. When David saw Saul sleeping, he quietly approached him and cut off Saul's robe, but he would not kill the king because Saul was one of God's anointed men. Saul was grateful for David's kindness and said to him, "You are more righteous than I; for you have repaid me good, whereas I have repaid you evil." And Saul took his men and went home.

Then David spoke to God and asked if he and his men should go up into the cities of Judah. And God told David that he should go to the city of Hebron in Judah. So David took his men and moved to Hebron, and the leaders of Judah came and anointed David king over the house of Judah.

After Saul's death, all the tribes of Israel came to David at Hebron and said, "Behold, we are your bone and flesh. God has said you shall be king over Israel." And the people of Israel anointed David to be their king.

Then King David brought the Ark of God to Jerusalem, and there was great rejoicing in the city. And so it was that from the city of Jerusalem, David ruled over Israel and Judah for thirty-three years.

SOLOMON

When David became too old to rule, he chose his son Solomon to take his place. The small kingdoms of Israel and Judah, over which Solomon ruled, needed strong allies in order to survive. The great Egyptian Empire to the south also needed a friendly neighbor. So Pharaoh gave his daughter in marriage to Solomon, to establish friendship and peace between the two countries.

Solomon knew that in addition to the military strength of a strong ally like Egypt, he, himself, must be a good ruler. So he prayed to God for the strength and wisdom to lead his people and to know the difference between good and evil. Solomon's prayers pleased God, and He told Solomon, "Because you have asked this, and have not asked for yourself long life or riches, I will make you wiser than any other man. I will give you also what you have not asked, both riches and honor, so that no other king shall compare with you."

God gave Solomon wisdom and understanding beyond measure, so that indeed no man compared to him. One day two women came to King Solomon. Both women were very upset, and one of them said to

64

the king, "This woman and I live in the same house. I gave birth to a son and three days later this woman also gave birth to a son. One night this woman's son died, and she arose while I was sleeping and stole my child, and laid her dead son at my side." Then the other woman said, "No, the living child is mine, and the dead child is yours." And the two women began to argue.

Solomon quieted the women and said to his servant, "Bring me a sword." When the servant returned with the sword, the king said to him, "Divide the child in two and give half to one woman and half to the other."

The second woman agreed. "It shall be neither mine nor yours," she said; "divide it." The first woman, however, whose son it *really* was, could not bear to see the child killed. She begged the king, "Oh my lord, give her the living child, and by no means slay it."

King Solomon saw that the first woman loved her son and would rather give him up than see him harmed, while the other woman was simply jealous of her. Then the king said to his servant, "Give the living child to the first woman, and by no means slay it, for she is the mother."

All of Israel heard of King Solomon's judgement, and they admired him because they saw that the wisdom of God was in him, helping him to give justice. He wrote songs and spoke over a thousand proverbs, which are short sayings that teach a lesson about life.

As God also promised, Solomon became the wealthiest king in the land. People came from all over to bring Solomon gifts and to listen to his wisdom. One of the king's visitors was the famous queen of Sheba, who had heard of Solomon's greatness. She came to see him for herself and to test him with hard questions. King Solomon amazed her by answering all of them, and she admired Solomon and marveled at the greatness and splendor of his kingdom.

King Hiram of Tyre, who had been a friend of David's, also admired Solomon and made a treaty of friendship with him. When Solomon prepared to build a great Temple to God as his father, David, had wished,

he obtained from King Hiram the materials he needed in exchange for wheat and oil.

The Temple was built with the finest cedar wood from the forest of Lebanon. The walls were carved with figures of angels, palm trees, and flowers. The inside of the sanctuary and the altar were covered with pure gold.

When the great Temple was finished, Solomon gathered his people for worship and brought the Ark of the Covenant, the Laws of God, into the "Holy of Holies". Here Solomon prayed with his people for God's guidance in knowing right from wrong; God's protection against the enemies of the Israelites; and God's forgiveness when the people sinned, for Solomon knew that no man was perfect.

After the people had gone home, God appeared to Solomon for the second time and said, "I have heard your prayer and I have blessed this house which you have built for me. If you will do all I have commanded you, then I will establish your royal throne over Israel forever."

But even Solomon, who was blessed with great wisdom, was not a perfect king. God had warned the Israelites not to marry anyone from a nation that worshipped idols, because He knew that the people would be tempted to worship idols themselves. As the years passed, Solomon married many women who were from nations that worshipped idols. And just as God had predicted, Solomon, himself, was tempted by these women and turned to worship other gods.

God became very angry with Solomon and told him that as punishment for his sins, He would deliver Solomon into the hands of his enemies, and Solomon's sons would *not* inherit the land. However, God did not forget the good things that Solomon had done. And he promised that some day Solomon's descendants would inherit the land again.

ELIJAH

After the death of King Solomon, most of the people in Israel turned to worshipping idols as Solomon had done. Yet there was one man who remained dedicated to God and served as His prophet; the man's name was Elijah.

Elijah visited Ahab, who was then the king of the Israelites, and warned him that if he continued to worship idols, God would take rain away from the land and cause a famine. Ahab was so angry at these words that he threatened Elijah's life, and forced him to flee from the kingdom.

Then God spoke to Elijah and told him to turn eastward and hide himself by a certain brook near the Jordan River. Here Elijah settled, and every morning and evening ravens brought bread and meat for him.

Elijah stayed by the brook until it dried up. Just as Elijah had warned Ahab, there came a day when God took rain away from the land, and even Elijah was forced to look for food and water. Once again, God

68

guided His prophet. He told him to go to the city of Zarephath, where he would find food and lodging with a widow and her son.

When Elijah arrived at the gate of the city, he saw a woman gathering sticks. He called to her and asked her to bring him some water and a piece of bread. The woman was reluctant to bring Elijah food. And she explained to him that all she had was a small amount of meal in a jar and a little drop of oil to burn.

Then Elijah said to the woman, "Don't be afraid. Make me a little cake from the meal and then make some for your son and yourself, for God will not let your jar become empty, and your oil shall not fail." The poor woman did as Elijah had commanded, and the prophet remained as a guest in her home for many days. During this time, to the woman's great surprise and joy, the jar of meal never became empty, and the oil continued to burn.

After many days had passed, God visited Elijah again and told him to return to King Ahab, because God was going to remove the famine from the land and send rain.

When Ahab saw Elijah, he greeted him in anger. He accused the prophet of bringing trouble to the land. But Elijah answered that Ahab and the people of Israel had brought trouble upon themselves, by worshipping false idols and disobeying God's commandments.

Elijah told Ahab to gather the people of Israel at Mount Carmel, where he would prove Ahab's idols to be false, worthless gods. When the people gathered at Mount Carmel, Elijah instructed the prophets of the idol Baal, to bring two bulls and to prepare one of these bulls as a sacrifice to God. Then Elijah said to the prophets of Baal, "Call on the name of your god and I will call on the name of the Lord; and the God who answers by fire, He *is* God." The prophets of Baal did as Elijah said, and called from morning until noon, and still there was no answer from their god.

It was then that Elijah asked all the people to come near the altar of God. Then he prayed, "O Lord, God of Abraham, Isaac and Israel, let it be known this day that thou art God in Israel." Then God answered with fire, as Elijah had asked, and the fire consumed the sacrifice. When the people of Israel saw God's answer in fire, they fell on their faces and said, "The Lord, He is God!" And they left their idols and returned in faith to the God of Elijah.

However, King Ahab continued to defy God by worshipping idols and committing evil acts. Ahab and his wife Jezebel thought only of their own gain, and they hurt everyone who got in their way. It so happened that Ahab wanted his neighbor's vineyard to use as a vegetable garden. When the neighbor refused, because the vineyard was his inheritance, Ahab and Jezebel had the man killed. God saw Ahab's injustice and sent

Elijah with an angry message for the king. The message was that just as Ahab and Jezebel gave death to their neighbor, so would they die by the hand of God. Then Ahab tore his clothes and put on a sack cloth, as a sign of humility and repentance for his sins.

Elijah continued to serve God as a prophet, and when he grew old, God instructed him to anoint a young man named Elisha to take his place. Elijah visited Elisha in the fields and placed his robe on the young man's shoulders; then Elijah blessed him as God's servant. And Elisha prayed that he might serve God with the same strong, unfailing spirit as that of the great prophet Elijah.

71

ELISHA

Elisha showed the power of God to the people, by healing the sick and performing miracles.

Once when Elisha was visiting in the city of Jericho, some men came to him for advice because a spring of water in their city was poisoned. The men explained that they did not want to move from Jericho, as the city was very pleasant and in a fine location. Elisha asked the men to bring him a bowl of salt, which he threw into the poisoned water. Through the power of God, the water immediately became clear and safe to drink.

Another time a woman in great distress came to Elisha. She told him that her husband was dead and that she had no money to pay her debts. To make matters worse, her creditor threatened to take her two children as slaves. Elisha asked the woman what she had in her house to give to

the creditor. The woman replied that she had nothing but a jar of oil. Elisha told her to borrow as many empty jars as she could from her neighbors, and to pour her own oil into the empty jars. To the woman's surprise, there was an endless supply of oil in her jar, and she was able to fill all the empty ones. Elisha then told her to sell the oil so that she could pay her debts.

Elisha traveled a lot. Whenever he passed through the city of Shunem, a wealthy woman prepared a room for him and invited Elisha to join her husband and herself. Elisha wanted to repay this woman's kindness, and when he saw that she was childless, he told her that God would give her a son in the springtime. When spring came, Elisha's words proved to be true, and the woman who had been childless for so long bore a son.

The child was healthy and grew into a sturdy infant. Then one day he suddenly became very ill and died. The heartbroken mother immediately called for Elisha, who prayed to God that the little boy be restored to life. After praying Elisha gently touched the child's hands, and to everyone's amazement, the boy sneezed seven times and opened his eyes. The boy's grateful mother fell to her knees and thanked God for His goodness and mercy.

Then Elisha went to Gilgal where there was a famine and food was very scarce. As Elisha sat with the sons of the Prophets, he asked his servant to prepare some soup. While dinner was being prepared, one of the men went into the field to gather herbs to put in the soup, and by mistake collected a poisonous wild vine. As soon as the men tasted the soup they cried to Elisha, "Oh man of God, there is death in the pot." So Elisha sprinkled some meal into the soup, and with God's power the poison was removed.

Gradually the famine was relieved in the land, and one day a man from a nearby city visited Elisha, bringing him the first fruits and twenty loaves of bread. Elisha told his servant to give the bread to his men. But the servant replied, saying, "How can I give twenty loaves of bread to one hundred men?" And Elisha told him, "There shall even be some left

over, for it is God's word." Then the men ate until they were full, and as God had predicted, still there was bread on the table.

Elisha had a reputation for being able to heal the sick. One day Naaman, an officer in the Syrian army, came to Elisha because he had leprosy, an incurable disease. Elisha advised Naaman to wash himself in the Jordan River seven times, and then he would be cured of the disease. Naaman thought this advice was silly, but his servants urged him to obey the man of God. Naaman went into the Jordan River and washed himself seven times as Elisha had instructed. When Naaman came out of the water, his flesh was as healthy as a child's, and the disease was gone. Then Naaman stood before his men and said, "Behold, I know that there is no God in all the earth but in Israel."

Elisha's followers grew in number, and when they became too large for their camp, they moved down to the Jordan River. While they were felling trees to build their homes, one of the men's axeheads fell in the river. The man was unhappy, not only because he had lost the axehead, but because he had borrowed the axe from a friend. The unhappy man took his problem to Elisha, who told him to cut off a stick and throw it into the river where the axehead had fallen. The man did this, and to his surprise, the iron axehead floated to the surface. He reached out his hand and took it in.

After some years had passed Elisha came to the city of Damascus, where the king of Syria was sick. The king sent his servant Hazael to meet the man of God, to ask if the illness could be cured. Elisha told Hazael that the king would soon die, and in his place Hazael would become king of Syria. Then Elisha looked very sadly into Hazael's eyes and began to weep. When Hazael asked Elisha why he wept, the man of God replied that he knew that one day Syria and Israel would fight each other, and thousands of lives would be lost.

Elisha's prophecy proved to be true. During the reign of Hazael, Syria went to war with Israel. King Joash was the ruler of Israel during this troubled time. One day, when Elisha knew that he was dying, he called the king to his bedside. There Elisha told Joash to draw his bow and shoot an arrow out of the window. When the king had done this, Elisha told him, "This is the arrow of victory, for you shall fight the Syrians until you have made an end to them." Next, he told Joash to take the arrows and strike the ground with them. The king of Israel struck the ground three times only and stopped. Elisha was angry with him and said, "You should have struck five or six times; then you would have struck down Syria until you had finally won, but now you will win only three times." Elisha knew that this would not be enough for complete victory, and that Joash was not forceful enough to overcome Israel's enemies.

EZRA

After the fall of Jerusalem and the destruction of the great Temple, the leaders of the people who were still alive were carried off to captivity in Babylon. Here they lived in exile for many years. In time Babylon, "the mighty city," was in its turn captured by the Persian king, Cyrus the Great, who tried to establish peace and prosperity in the many conquered countries that he ruled. He permitted the people living in Jerusalem to rebuild the city and the Temple, and promised that the treasures of the Lord would be restored to Jerusalem.

Following the rebuilding of the Temple, Cyrus the Great put a priest named Ezra in charge of the Temple. The king also granted him permission to lead another group of exiles back to Jerusalem, in order to dedicate the treasures. The generous king Cyrus also gave Ezra gold and silver, and money with which to buy bulls and lambs to sacrifice to God.

So Ezra began to prepare for the return to Jerusalem. Outside the city, on the shore of a stream named the Ahava, the band of exiles camped

for three days to organize the caravan. Ezra went among them to make sure that all the leaders of the Israelites were with him. But he found that no Levites were there. Many of the exiles preferred to stay in Babylon, where they had become settled, rather than make the long, hard journey back to Jerusalem. The Levites were a special priestly group who were appointed to help take care of the Temple. Because Ezra wished to serve God well, he recruited thirty-eight of these men to go with him to check the treasure, and guard it, since they were men set apart for this task.

Ezra then asked his people to fast for one day to show their reverence and to pray to God for protection during their journey. For Ezra knew that there were many enemies along the way, who would try to ambush them. The caravan finally arrived safely in Jerusalem with all the vessels of gold and silver, which were placed in the Temple in devotion to God. Then the high priest took the bulls and lambs and gave them to God as a sacrifice.

Shortly after the treasures had been dedicated, officials of the Temple brought Ezra bad news. The people who had been living in Jerusalem before Ezra and his men had returned there were freely mixing with nations that worshipped idols. And they were also entering into marriages with strangers who did not serve God. When Ezra heard this, he was deeply troubled. For he knew that this time no enemies had prevented his people from worshipping God; they had simply turned away from God, through their own wilfulness and disobedience.

Ezra fell to his knees in prayer and wept bitterly for all the people who had proved so faithless. While Ezra was praying, a great assembly of men, women and children gathered around him. And one of the men stepped forward to speak to him. He told Ezra that there was *still* hope in Israel, for some of the people knew what God had done for them. These people agreed to separate themselves from the idol-worshippers and return to God. Ezra came forward and made the people take an oath, pledging themselves to do what they had promised — which was to send the idolators away from Jerusalem and to be obedient to God's will.

NEHEMIAH

Ezra and his followers rebuilt the Temple in Jerusalem, but the great wall that had once surrounded the city and protected the Israelites was still broken down. This was dangerous, as it was the time of frequent small wars, and revolts against the rule of a great king in a distant city.

The Israelites had been favored by the Persian ruler; he had ended their captivity, allowed them to return to their homes and rebuild the Temple, and he had restored the treasures to the House of the Lord. Because they were loyal to the Persian king, the people in Jerusalem were often attacked. But they had no defense against the raids and plundering of their warring, pagan neighbors, because of the broken wall.

Travellers from Judah brought word to the court of the Persian King, Artaxerxes, of the terrible distress of the defenseless people in Jerusalem. One of the highest-ranking officials of the royal court was Nehemiah, who had risen from the group of exiles to become the king's cup-bearer. When Nehemiah heard of the suffering of his fellow Israelites in Jerusalem, he wept and prayed and mourned so greatly that the king asked him what the trouble was. He told the king that the city — the place of his fathers' tombs — lay in waste, and the gates were burned down. Nehemiah then asked the king to send him to Judah, to the city of Jerusalem, to rebuild it. Artaxerxes granted this request and gave him passports and letters of authority which made him the royal governor.

When Nehemiah arrived in Jerusalem he spent three days learning about the situation. Then, taking only a few men, he went out to inspect the broken walls at night. He did this secretly because he did not want his enemies to know about his plan to rebuild the fortifications, lest they

attack while the defenses were weakened. When he knew what had to be done, he gathered the workers needed for the construction. Craftsmen and merchants from the city neighborhoods, farmers and workers from the nearby towns, even the priests from the Temple, all came to join in this great undertaking.

At first the enemies of the Israelites ridiculed Nehemiah and his men, for attempting so great a task. But when they saw how the walls grew, they became very angry and plotted together to attack and stop the work. Nehemiah prayed to God and kept his men at work. In addition each worker kept his weapons at his side, and those who were not at work guarded the others. This show of force discouraged the enemies, and so the workers finished the walls and the gates and the towers, and all that was needed to make the city safe.

When this great task was done, Nehemiah gathered all the people to join in a great procession — the priests, their assistants, the Levites, who sang and played the musical instruments, and the community leaders. All of them marched around the walls and passed the great gates, to give thanks and to dedicate the walls to God.

Nehemiah, his assignment completed, returned to the court of King Artaxerxes. After staying there for a while, he went to Jerusalem again and found that things were not as good as when he had left. The people were not prosperous and they had neglected to make their offerings to God at the Temple. The priests had become careless, and a man named Tobiah had even moved his furniture into one of the Temple chambers. Nehemiah was very angry and made Tobiah move his possessions out of the Holy place. Then he brought the people back to worship at the Temple, as the Lord had commanded.

There were also other reforms that had to be made. Many people were working, selling, and doing many other things on the Sabbath; others were breaking God's laws by marrying idol-worshippers. Nehemiah stopped all these sins so that the people of Israel might truly worship God and obey His laws.

ESTHER

In the days of the Old Testament there lived a rich and power-ful king named Ahasuerus, who ruled all of the Persian Empire. To celebrate his great prosperity, King Ahasuerus invited his princes, noblemen and servants to a big feast, which lasted for seven days.

On the last day of the celebration, the King sent for his beautiful wife Vashti, because he was proud of her and wanted to present her to the people. But Vashti refused to come at the King's command. Ahasuerus was enraged at the queen's rude behavior and felt that her actions might encourage other wives to disobey their husbands. So he sent Vashti away from the palace and issued a decree. This called all the beautiful young maidens of the land to come before him, so that he could choose a new queen.

A Jew named Mordecai heard the decree and was eager for his niece Esther to go before the King, because she was very beautiful. So Mor-decai brought Esther to the palace, first advising her not to tell anyone that she was of the house of Israel.

When Esther went before Ahasuerus, he could not take his eyes away from her. He fell in love with her and preferred her to all the other maidens. So he set the royal crown on Esther's head and made her queen in place of Vashti.

After several days had passed, Esther's uncle Mordecai happened to pass two of the King's guards and overheard them plotting to murder the King. Immediately Mordecai went to Esther, who in turn told Ahasuerus of the plan to murder him. When the matter was investigated, the two guards confessed to the plot and were put to death.

Then Ahasuerus appointed a man named Haman, in whom he had great trust, to be his chief officer in charge of the many princes and governors in the land. All the people of Persia bowed down to Haman, to show their respect for the King's favored servant. But Mordecai did not trust Haman and refused to bow down to him. Haman was filled with fury and hatred and vowed that he would punish not only Mordecai, but all the Jews in the land.

Haman went to Ahasuerus with an untrue story. He told the King that certain people in Persia were following their own customs, instead of obeying the King's laws. Haman urged the King to destroy these people, because he said they were weakening his kingdom. Ahasuerus trusted and believed Haman. And so he gave him full permission to do whatever he believed was necessary, for the good of the country. With the King's permission, the evil Haman ordered the death of every Jew in the land.

When Mordecai heard this fearful news, he tore his clothes and put on sack cloth, the robes of grief. Then he went to Esther's chambermaids and asked them to take the news to Esther. He also told them to ask her to go before the King and plead for her people's safety, and for her own life.

However, there was a royal custom that no one could approach the King unless that person was sent for. If any man or woman disobeyed this rule, the penalty was death. But Esther knew that she had to speak to the King, not only to save her own life, but for the sake of all the Jews in

Persia. So she put on her most beautiful royal robes and stood at the entrance to the King's palace. Ahasuerus was sitting on his throne, and he at once saw his fair queen standing before him. Instead of being angry, Ahasuerus was pleased to see her and held out his golden sceptre to show Esther that she was welcome. And Esther drew near and touched the end of the sceptre, as a sign of respect to the King.

Then Ahasuerus promised to grant any wish for Esther, even if it meant giving away half of his kingdom. But Esther explained that her only wish at that moment was for the King and his officer Haman to join her at dinner the next evening. Both the King and Haman accepted Esther's invitation, and Haman went away feeling very happy and honored that the queen had chosen him as her guest. In fact, he felt so safe and sure of both the King and Queen's favor, that he had the gallows made for Mordecai's hanging the next morning.

That same evening, King Ahasuerus had trouble falling asleep. So he sent for a special book in which all the memorable deeds in the land were recorded. As Ahasuerus was reading, he came to the part which told how Mordecai had saved his life, by exposing the murderous plot of the two royal guards. Ahasuerus asked his servants if any honor or reward had been given to Mordecai. And they replied that nothing had been done for him. Just then, Haman entered the King's chamber to speak to Ahasuerus about Mordecai's hanging, as the gallows was prepared. But before Haman could say anything, Ahasuerus asked his trusted officer, "What shall be done to the man whom the King delights to honor?" And Haman, thinking that the King wanted to honor him, said, "I would give this man royal robes that the King has worn, a horse that the King has ridden, and let him ride through the streets of the city for all the people to honor." Then King Ahasuerus said to Haman, "Make haste, take the robes and the horse, as you have said, and do so to Mordecai the Jew who sits at the King's gate." Haman was shocked by the King's request, but he obeyed Ahasuerus. In great anger and jealousy, he led Mordecai through the streets to be honored by the whole city.

The next evening, Ahasuerus and Haman attended Queen Esther's feast. While everyone was eating, the King said to Esther, "What is your wish?" And Esther replied, "My wish is that you save the lives of my people and myself, for we have been ordered to die." Then King Ahasuerus said, "Who is this man who could do such a thing?" Again Esther replied, "A foe and an enemy! This wicked Haman! He has ordered the death of all the Jews, and since I am a Jew, I am to die too." Angrily King Ahasuerus rose to his feet and ordered Haman to be hanged from the very gallows he had prepared for Mordecai.

Then Ahasuerus gave Haman's house to Queen Esther, and chose Mordecai to be his chief officer in place of Haman.

When the Jews heard of this victory against the villainous Haman who threatened to take their lives, they all gathered and made an enormous feast. To this day, every year the Jews celebrate a holiday called Purim, at which time this ancient story of Esther is retold.

The Bible has many, many stories about the way in which God guided and helped the leaders of His people, and of the way God talked to those who faithfully believed in Him and tried to obey His Commands.

In the beginning God spoke directly to those who served Him, and who brought His words to mankind. Later, as men became more involved in their own lives and in the world around them, they became more remote from God. And so He chose certain persons to bring His message to all men. Among these chosen spokesmen were a group called Prophets. Their sayings and deeds were written down, and each Prophet had a book named after him.

ISAIAH

In the kingdom of Judah there lived a young man named Isaiah. One day he had a vision of God sitting upon a throne surrounded by His seraphim and all the heavenly host. God called to Isaiah and asked him to be His prophet, a spokesman for God, but Isaiah felt that he was unworthy. Then one of the seraphim flew to Isaiah, touched the young man's mouth with a burning firestone from the altar of sacrifice and said, "Behold, this has touched your lips; your guilt is taken away."

At this time King Ahaz of Judah was worried, because the Syrians and other nearby nations had joined together to wage war on Jerusalem. But God sent His prophet to encourage and reassure Ahaz. Isaiah arranged to meet Ahaz outside the city walls, beyond the protection of the fortifications and the army. He did this to show Ahaz that he must depend first upon God for strength and courage, not upon his military might for protection. Ahaz was told that if he did not trust God he would not be secure. Ahaz agreed to put his faith in God's word and later, as God had promised, the Israelites defeated the Syrians and their allies.

When King Ahaz died, his son Hezekiah took his place. During Hezekiah's reign, the king of Assyria sent a messenger to tell the Israelites that the Assyrians were coming to take over their country. The messenger told the people that their God was powerless, and that Hezekiah was deceiving them when he entrusted their safety to God. The messenger also urged the Israelites to surrender peacefully and promised that they would be treated well.

When Hezekiah heard the words of the Assyrian messenger, he tore his clothes and covered himself with sack-cloth as a sign of grief. He prayed to God that his people would not listen to the Assyrian, who had mocked God and threatened to destroy the kingdoms of Judah and Israel.

Then Hezekiah asked Isaiah to pray for God's help. And Isaiah predicted that God would not let the Assyrians take over the land. For God had revealed to him a new plan, whereby He was going to build Judah and Israel into strong nations so that they could defend themselves.

The same night that Isaiah spoke his reassurance, God stopped the Assyrians from entering Jerusalem. Thousands died in the camp outside the city, and those that remained alive fled.

Shortly after this Hezekiah became very ill and was at the point of death. Isaiah came and said to the king, "Thus says the Lord, 'Set your house in order; for you shall die soon.'" When Hezekiah heard these words, he turned his face to the wall and wept bitterly. He prayed to God to grant him longer life, since he had been a faithful servant and a good man. Then as Isaiah was about to leave the king's house, God called him and said, "Turn back and tell Hezekiah that I have heard his prayer and have seen his tears, and I will add fifteen years to his life."

At God's command, Isaiah sent for a poultice of figs and placed them on Hezekiah's sore. Then, as a sign that the king would be cured, God made the shadow on the sun dial go ten degrees backward; in other words He made the day longer. As God had promised, Hezekiah soon grew healthy and strong and blessed Isaiah for bringing the word of God to him.

Hezekiah was indeed a good and great king, who sought to abolish the worship of idols and pagan shrines, and lead the Israelites victoriously against their oppressors.

Isaiah was looking forward to the coming of the Messiah. At that time the people would be able to turn their swords into ploughshares and their spears into pruning hooks; to farm the land instead of using it as a battleground.

JEREMIAH

In the land of Benjamin in Israel, there lived a boy named Jeremiah. One day God appeared to him and appointed him to be His prophet, to travel through the land and bring the word of God to the people. Jeremiah was afraid and said to God, "I am just a young boy, and I don't know how to speak to the people." God touched Jeremiah's lips and said, "Behold, I have put My words in your mouth." Then Jeremiah saw an almond tree just bursting into bloom. This reminded him that the rod of an almond tree was a symbol of punishment and he knew this was a sign that the people were risking God's judgment for their wicked ways.

Once again, in Israel the people had turned away from God and begun to worship the idol Baal. Of course, an idol had no power to understand and guide the Israelites, for it was simply a stone image. Without God's guidance the Israelites became a weak, evil people. They stole from their neighbors; they practiced slavery; they slaughtered innocent people through unnecessary wars.

God's anger grew, for even His priests began to worship the stone images. When God could no longer tolerate the people's faithlessness and wickedness, He called Jeremiah and instructed the prophet to put on a linen waistcloth. After Jeremiah had done this, God told him to take off the waistcloth and hide it between the rocks along the river. Several days passed, and then God told Jeremiah to go back to the river and take the waistcloth from its hiding place. When Jeremiah looked at the cloth, he saw that it was ruined and worthless. And then God said to him, "These evil people who refuse to hear My words, who stubbornly follow other gods, shall be like this waistcloth which is good for nothing; for I will destroy the people who are evil."

God then told Jeremiah to go down to the potter's house, to watch

the man make his earthenware vessels. Jeremiah saw that as the potter worked with the soft clay, he could either build or destroy the article in his hand. Then God said to Jeremiah, "Behold, like the clay in the potter's hand, so is the House of Israel in My hand. If the people are evil, I will destroy their nation, and if they repent and do good, I will rebuild their nation."

For many years Jeremiah brought the word of God to his people. Some listened and obeyed God's laws, but others continued to worship idols and disobey the Ten Commandments. An Israelite priest named Pashur, who disagreed with Jeremiah's prophecies, beat him and put him in the stocks, a wooden frame that held the prisoner's head and wrists. But the next morning, when Pashur released him from the stocks, Jeremiah told the priest that God would punish him and Israel by delivering them into the hands of their enemies, the Babylonians.

After several years had passed, God visited Jeremiah and said, "Take a scroll and write on it all the words that I have spoken to you, so that all the Israelites may turn from evil in time to save themselves." Then Jeremiah asked his faithful friend Baruch to write down the words of God, as Jeremiah dictated them.

When the prophecies had been written down, Jeremiah told Baruch to read them in the Temple before all the Israelites. For Jeremiah could not read his own prophecies, because the idol-worshippers had barred him from the Temple. But Baruch did as Jeremiah had said, and read them to the people.

When Jehoiakim, the king of Israel, heard about the written prophecies, he sent for the scroll and had one of his men read to him. As the reader came to the end of a passage, Jehoiakim cut it off with his knife and threw it into the fire, until finally Jeremiah's entire scroll was destroyed.

Then God appeared to Jeremiah in great fury and told him to write another scroll, and God also promised that none of Jehoiakim's descendants would sit upon the throne.

94

As God had promised, a man named Zedekiah was made king instead of Jehoiakim's son, but neither he nor the people of the land listened to the words of God, which He spoke through his prophet Jeremiah. So God told Jeremiah that He was sending the Babylonians to attack Jerusalem.

When the prophet warned the Israelites that the Babylonians were coming, they refused to believe him. It was then that Jeremiah prepared to leave Jerusalem, to return to Benjamin, the land of his birth. When the prophet arrived at the gates of the city the king's guards stopped him and accused him of going to help the enemy. Jeremiah protested, but the guards did not believe him. They beat him and threw him into a dungeon where he remained for many days. When the rest of the people heard that Jeremiah had been caught, they demanded that he be cast into a deep, dark pit to punish him further. Here the prophet remained until the king's servant, an Ethiopian, brought Zedekiah the news that Jeremiah was dying of hunger.

The king feared Jeremiah for his predictions about the fate of the Israelites. He was also afraid that God would take revenge upon *him,* if he let the prophet die. So he ordered his men to draw Jeremiah from the pit and bring him to the palace. Here Zedekiah questioned the prophet about his predictions and asked if there were any way to escape God's anger. Jeremiah told him that God's command was firm and that the Babylonians would burn Jerusalem to the ground.

It came to pass as Jeremiah had prophesied. King Nebuchadnezzar of Babylonia came with his army, broke down the great walls of Jerusalem, and burned the city to the ground. Then he took Zedekiah and the Israelite prisoners back to his kingdom, where they were kept in bondage for many years.

Nebuchadnezzar, however, treated Jeremiah kindly for he recognized the prophet's wisdom and knew that God was with him. The king ordered his men to listen to all of Jeremiah's words and to take him back to Benjamin, the land of his birth.

EZEKIEL

God first appeared to Ezekiel as a great brightness that lit up the heavens. When Ezekiel saw the powerful light, he fell upon his face, and God said to him, "Son of man, stand upon your feet, for I am going to send you to Israel, a nation that has sinned against me to this very day."

Ezekiel was told that he was to prophesy, to bring the words of the Lord to the people, even if they mocked him or refused to listen. God handed him a scroll on which words of sorrow and mourning were written. As Ezekiel read the scroll, he memorized each word and knew that the Spirit of God was with him. Then, with a rumbling sound like a great earthquake, God left him.

Ezekiel went down among the Israelite exiles who lived along the Chebar River in Babylonia. There he spoke to the people and asked them to turn from their wicked ways and their idol worship. Some of them listened to him, while others stubbornly refused.

Then God instructed Ezekiel to take a big clay tile and draw the city

of Jerusalem on it. When the prophet had made his drawing, God told him to add enemy camps and battering rams around the city wall, as a sign to the people that one day Israel would be destroyed completely.

As another sign of Israel's fate, God had Ezekiel shave his head, cut off his beard, and then scatter his hair into the wind in every direction. God was saying that as Ezekiel had shaved and scattered his hair, so would God destroy the nation of Israel and scatter the survivors all over the land.

Some time after this, Ezekiel saw another vision of God. This time God lifted the prophet and carried him to the city of Jerusalem, where he was able to see all the sins of the people. God brought him into the Temple and showed him the idol that the people were worshipping, then He took him down into a secret chapel where seventy leaders of the city were worshipping a wall of carved beasts and reptiles.

When Ezekiel had seen the sins of Israel, God ordered him to hire six executioners to slaughter every man, woman and child who followed wickedness or worshipped idols. Ezekiel sent a man to mark the forehead of every person who regretted and grieved over the evil of Israel. And when this had been done, he sent the six executioners through the city of Jerusalem, telling them to spare everyone with a mark upon his forehead, but to show no mercy to the rest of the people. The men obeyed Ezekiel's command, slaying a great number and sparing a few people. Thus, at the end of his vision, Ezekiel knew that only the few who followed God's laws would be saved.

Israel succumbed to the power of her enemies and eventually dissolved. The survivors were captured and scattered throughout the land just as God had promised, and as Ezekiel had seen in his visions.

Then Ezekiel had another vision about the fall of Tyre, a proud, rich nation that had helped to destroy Jerusalem. Tyre bordered on the sea and was known for her beautiful ships and her commerce with distant lands. Although there was fabulous wealth, the people were selfish and wanted only profits for themselves. Ezekiel foresaw that the ships would sink and all the cargo would be destroyed. Without ships, Tyre would lose all her wealth and power.

Ezekiel had yet another vision, this time about the rebuilding of Israel. The Spirit of God came to him and showed him a valley full of dry bones. Here God said to him, "Prophesy to these bones and say that I will cause breath to enter them and they shall live." Ezekiel prophesied as he was commanded, and when he finished, there was a noise and a great rattling. Suddenly the bones came together with flesh and skin upon them, but no breath in them. At God's command Ezekiel called to the four winds to breathe upon the bodies so that they might live. When he was done, breath came into the bodies and they stood on their feet and lived.

God then told Ezekiel that the bones were a symbol of the house of Israel. One day, just as He had done in the vision, God would gather the people who were scattered in other nations and reunite them in their own land.

DANIEL

King Nebuchadnezzar kept the Israelites captive in Babylonia for many years. During this time the king chose some of the brighter Israelite youths from royal or noble families, and educated them. The king ordered that the young men be served the same kind of food and wine as the royal household. Now the Israelites had special dietary laws that permitted them to eat only certain foods. Because of these laws, one of the youths, named Daniel, refused to eat the king's rich food. Instead, he asked Nebuchadnezzar's servant to give him and his friends only vegetables and water. The servant was willing, but afraid such a diet would weaken their health. So Daniel suggested a trial of the two diets for ten days. At the end of the ten days, the servant saw that Daniel and his friends were stronger and sturdier than the youths who ate the king's rich food. Because they had obeyed the laws, God had favored them and from then on Daniel's words were highly valued in court.

God gave to these favored young men great wisdom and skill in writing, but to Daniel, God gave a special ability to understand visions and dreams.

In the second year of his rule, Nebuchadnezzar was troubled by many dreams and could not get to sleep. He called for his magicians and said to them, "I had a strange dream and my spirit is troubled to know the meaning of it." The magicians replied, "Tell us what the dream is and we will tell you its meaning." Nebuchadnezzar grew angry and said, "If you are really magicians, you will be able to tell me what my dream is, as well as what it means." He told his wise men that if they granted his request, he would give them gifts and great honor. But if they failed to tell him the dream or lied about its meaning, he would put them to death. The magicians trembled in fear and told Nebuchadnezzar that the task was impossible.

The king then ordered Daniel and his companions to put the magicians to death. When Daniel heard this severe command, he prayed that God might let him know the mystery of Nebuchadnezzar's dream so that he might save these wise men. That night God visited Daniel in a vision and revealed to him the meaning of the dream.

The next day Daniel went to see Nebuchadnezzar and told him that no wise men, magicians, or astrologers could understand his dream, for this was a task that only God could perform. Then Daniel told the king what God had revealed the night before. The dream was about things

100

that would happen in the future. In the dream the king stood before a mighty statue of blinding brightness, and it frightened him. The head was gold, the chest and arms of silver, the belly and thighs of bronze, the legs of iron, and the feet of iron and clay. As the king looked at the image, a great stone appeared and struck the statue's feet, breaking them to pieces. And the rest of the statue crumbled into dust, so that not a trace of it could be found. But the stone that struck the image became a great mountain and filled the whole earth.

After Daniel had finished describing the dream, he explained to Nebuchadnezzar what it meant. Daniel said that the head of gold stood for Nebuchadnezzar and his kingdom. The parts of the statue that were of silver, bronze, iron, and clay represented other kingdoms, that would come after Nebuchadnezzar for many, many years. The stone which struck the image represented the kingdom set up by God in heaven, which would never be destroyed, and which would never lose its dominion, and which would fill the whole earth. Thus the great God had tried to show the king what was to come.

When Daniel finished, Nebuchadnezzar fell upon his face and paid tribute to the wise young man and said to him, "Truly your God is God of gods and Lord of kings and a revealer of mysteries; for you have been able to understand my dream." Then the king gave Daniel high honors and many great gifts, and made him chief over all the wise men in Babylonia.

When Nebuchadnezzar died, his son Belshazzar took his place as king of Babylonia and made a great feast for his lords. During the feast, Belshazzar commanded that his father's vessels of gold and silver be brought, so that wine could be drunk from them. As the people drank and enjoyed the wine, they praised the gods of gold and silver.

Suddenly the feast was interrupted when a man's hand appeared mysteriously and wrote on the wall of the palace. All those who saw the hand were frightened, because it appeared from nowhere. When the

hand finally disappeared, the words, "Mene, mene, tekel, upharsin" were left on the wall. Belshazzar was in a panic and sent for his wise men to interpret the strange writing, which no one at the feast could read. The king promised that whoever interpreted the words would be clothed in rich purple garments and wear a chain of gold around his neck.

Then the queen remembered Daniel, Nebuchadnezzar's wise man, and had him brought to the palace to quiet her husband's fears. Daniel looked at the writing on the wall and knew exactly where it came from and exactly what it meant. He told Belshazzar that God had sent the hand to condemn the king and his people, for praising the false gods of gold and silver and failing to honor the Lord. Daniel told the king that the word "mene" meant that God would destroy Belshazzar's kingdom in a number of days. "Tekel" meant that the king's actions had been weighed and were found lacking in goodness. "Upharsin" meant that Belshazzar's kingdom would be divided among the Medes and the Persians.

Belshazzar, as distressed as he was by Daniel's words, kept his promise and ordered Daniel to be clothed in royal robes and made him third ruler in the kingdom. That very same night King Belshazzar was slain and Darius the Mede captured the kingdom.

Darius set one hundred and twenty princes and three presidents, one of whom was Daniel, over his kingdom. Daniel was honored above all the other presidents and princes, because of his excellent spirit; in fact, Darius planned to set him over the whole kingdom one day. The rest of the leaders became very jealous of Daniel yet they could find no fault in him, nothing to make him lose his favor with the king. Since they could not find fault with Daniel, they decided to trick the king into putting him to death.

The leaders went to King Darius and advised him to strengthen his power over the people, by ordering them to leave their gods for thirty days and worship only the king. Anyone who disobeyed the command would be thrown into the lions' den. Darius was a vain man who enjoyed power, so he agreed to issue the foolish decree.

104

Although Daniel knew that the decree had been issued, he continued to worship God three times a day, as he had always done. The other leaders, who expected Daniel to disobey the king's order, spied on him and reported to the king that Daniel had broken the decree and must be punished. The king was greatly distressed when he heard that Daniel was a victim of his horrible decree and tried to excuse him. But the wicked men said: "The law of the Medes and the Persians is that no decree which the king has made may be changed."

So Daniel was thrown into the lions' den. The king said to him, "May your God, whom you serve continually, save you!" Then a stone was placed against the entrance of the den so that Daniel could not escape. Darius went back to his palace and could not eat or sleep because of his grief.

The next morning the king arose and went in haste to the den of lions. When he came near, he cried out, "Oh Daniel, has your God been able to save you from the lions?" To the king's surprise Daniel answered, "Oh king, live forever! My God sent his angel and shut the lions' mouths." Because Daniel had such faith in God, he was safely delivered from the lions' den.

The king ordered the men who had plotted against Daniel to be thrown into the lions' den themselves. Before they reached the bottom of the pit, the lions killed them, for the men had no God to protect them. King Darius then proclaimed that the God of Daniel was the living God whose kingdom would last forever.

After this Daniel prospered in the reign of Darius and in the reign of Cyrus the Persian.

HOSEA

God's word came to Hosea through personal sorrow, the tragedy of a broken home and an unfaithful love. He had found and married a woman who was among the evil people of the land, a woman named Gomer who cared only for her selfish desires. Soon after their marriage, Hosea's wife left him, and turned to other men who praised her beauty and offered her gifts of bread, wool, flax, and wine. Hosea was heartbroken and grieved for the wife he had lost and for the shame she had caused him and his children.

Then God spoke to Hosea and said, "Now you know my suffering. For as your wife has left you with grief and shame, so have My children Israel left Me to suffer by going to worship idols and following greed and lust instead of justice and righteousness."

After a while, the other men that Gomer had gone to grew tired of her and left her. When Hosea's unfaithful wife had eaten the bread, drunk the wine, and used the flax, oil, and wool, she realized that she was left with nothing. She became a slave and saw the great mistake she had made by trading her husband's love for worthless flattery and gifts that were quickly used.

Then God told Hosea to redeem his wife from slavery and forgive her, for she had learned her lesson and had repented for her sins. Hosea saw that this was a lesson for the people of Israel, too; that if they saw the worthlessness of their false gods and truly repented, God would redeem and love them.

JOEL

God sent his prophet Joel to preach at a time when there was a terrible plague in the land. Locusts came in great numbers, swarmed upon the fields, and devoured all the crops. The people of Israel were afraid they would all die of hunger, so they tore their clothes to show God that they were afraid of His ways and begged for mercy.

Joel went among the Israelites and told them that tearing their clothes was not enough. To satisfy God they would have to change their evil ways and lead good lives. He told them that they still had a chance to save themselves from total destruction, for God loved His children and wanted to see them grow strong. In order to be saved, all the people in the nation — the elders of the city, married couples, brides, grooms, children and infants — were to gather at a holy meeting. There each person would give up his selfishness and false idols, and accept the laws of one God. No one was to be left out. Joel knew that the Israelites must be brought together to repent, to worship with faithfulness in the temple the way God had taught them. He also knew that God would then take away the swarming locusts and restore grain to the fields and fruit to the vines. More than these rewards, however, Joel saw that in the dark night of need and despair, a turning to God would bring them all the blessings of peace and prosperity. For then the Lord would dwell among His people.

AMOS

A mos was a shepherd who lived in a small village of Tekoa, in the Judean hills. Like most of the other shepherds and farmers, he was a poor man.

One day God commanded Amos to go down to the prosperous city of Bethel where Jeroboam, the king of Israel lived. Amos was amazed when he saw the great contrast between the hard life of his friends in the country and the soft, luxurious life of the wealthy rulers and merchants in the city. And he knew that God wanted him to warn the people that all their power and wealth would be taken away, if they continued to be selfish and neglect the poor.

Amos reprimanded the people of Bethel for paying the farmers and shepherds so little for their grain and sheep. He told them that God did not want great feasts in His honor, or burnt offerings of the finest sheep and grain when other people did not have enough food. That kind of easy worship, without true obedience and thoughtfulness, would bring ultimate destruction on the foolish people.

Amaziah, the high priest of Bethel, confronted Amos and told him that reproaches had aroused the anger of King Jeroboam. He told Amos that he must leave the city and prophesy in another land. Amos replied that he was not a fortune-teller or a professional soothsayer, but a simple shepherd who felt the sorrow of the poor people and saw the evil in the land. Therefore, he would not leave the country or stop preaching until he had delivered God's message.

OBADIAH

God sent His prophet Obadiah to preach against the tribe of Edom for betraying Israel. The two tribes were neighbors and also relatives, because the people of Edom were descendants of Esau, and the people of Israel were descendants of Jacob, Esau's brother.

The Edomites lived high on the cliffs where no other tribe dared to bother them. When the Babylonians attacked Israel, the Edomites offered no help. They remained safely on their cliffs and rejoiced at the destruction of Jerusalem. After the city had been destroyed, some of the Edomites went down and stole whatever treasures remained. Then they stopped the Israelite survivors who were fleeing from the city and turned them over to the enemy.

Obadiah brought God's word to the Edomites and told them, "As you have done, it shall be done to you. Your deeds shall return upon your own head." The prophet told them that one day all the nations would unite and drive the proud people from their cliffs, so that not one man from the house of Esau would remain. And the people of Israel, the descendants of Jacob, would rise in power among the nations and rule the land.

JONAH

This is a parable or story about a man named Jonah who was chosen by God to preach to the people of Nineveh, which was a great city in a distant land. These people were not Hebrews and did not know about God's loving care and guidance. But Jonah did not really want to preach there. And so, hoping to escape God's command, he went to the coast and boarded a ship that was sailing in the opposite direction, toward the faraway city of Tarshish.

God knew everything that Jonah did, and after the prophet had been at sea for a few days, He sent a mighty storm that threatened to wreck the ship. All the crew members prayed to their gods, but Jonah realized that the storm was his punishment for trying to leave the presence of God.

Jonah then told the men what he had done and said to them, "Throw me into the sea, and then the storm will quiet down." The men pitied Jonah and were reluctant to throw him into the rough waters. Instead they rowed as hard as they could and tried to bring the ship back to land. The harder they rowed, however, the more the sea raged. Finally they saw that the only way to save themselves was to throw Jonah overboard. As soon as they had done so, the sea became calm and the storm ceased.

Jonah was tossed about in the sea, but he did not drown for God had appointed a great whale to swallow him. For three days and nights Jonah remained alive inside the fish, thinking about his disobedience and praying for God's forgiveness. When Jonah had been punished enough and was ready to go on with his mission, God caused the whale to open its mouth and deliver Jonah safely on dry land.

Jonah went on to Nineveh and so brought God's word to other people as well as the Israelites, thus showing His love for all nations.

114

MICAH

The prophet Micah rebuked the Israelites in Samaria and Jerusalem for failing to worship God and for breaking the Ten Commandments. In these two cities people grew rich by cheating their neighbors. Selfish kings took payment for giving help to needy people; wise men demanded rewards in return for their knowledge; and priests expected money for giving blessings.

The people of Samaria and Jerusalem knew that they had done wrong and asked Micah how they might please God. Should they bring Him burnt offerings of the best calves? Should they sacrifice their first-born children?

Micah replied that God did not want any of these things. Instead, He expected their faith and obedience; He wanted them to do justice, to be kind, and to respect God. Micah knew that if people did this, there would come a time when there would be peace in the land and no man would have to fear his neighbors. God's children would set an example for all. People would come from all over the world to God's Temple at Mount Zion and accept His laws.

NAHUM

For hundreds of years the Israelites and other nations remained captives of the Assyrians. The prisoners were forced to worship false gods; their homes, land, and possessions were taken from them.

The prophet Nahum had a vision and saw the fall of Nineveh, the richest, strongest city in Assyria. God appeared and told the prophet that Ninevah's good fortune would suddenly change, that Israel and other captive nations would fight and destroy the mighty empire of Assyria. All this Nahum wrote down in a long poem.

In his vision Nahum saw the great Assyrian army fleeing from Nineveh. Officers dressed in bright scarlet uniforms were trying to keep order among their men, but could not. Horses and chariots ran wild in the streets, and captives took over the royal palace. Nobles, princes, wise men fled with the rest of their people and scattered into the mountains. All those that lived by the sword perished.

God told Nahum that although the Assyrians were great in number, they would never unite again as a nation. He told him that the scattered exiles from Israel would band together and form their own nation once more. Nahum knew that his God ruled over all men and would maintain justice and supply the needs of His people.

HABAKKUK

During a time when Israel was constantly threatened by its powerful and war-like neighbors, a man named Habakkuk prayed to God and asked the question, "How long must Israel endure the destruction and the violence of its enemies?"

Habakkuk could not understand why evil men, who robbed the poor and took land that did not belong to them, triumphed over good, honest men.

God answered Habakkuk and told him that he must have patience. He said that in time the greedy people would destroy themselves, because they were never satisfied with what they had, and always wanted more. God also warned him that the number of captives would increase, until one day the prisoners would form a great army and turn against their greedy conquerors. The evil men who were once proud and powerful would be scorned and shamed. And they would never rise again. However, God did not indicate when all this would happen. Habakkuk, standing on a tower far above the city watching people come and go about their daily lives, thought about this question and the answer God had given him. Only then did he realize that God's time is not man's time; and that only the righteous survive and that they must live by their faith.

ZEPHANIAH

The people of Jerusalem had once again fallen into evil ways; their kings were obedient to foreign rulers, and they worshipped the pagan idols of their conquerors in addition to the God of Israel. Of course, this was a direct violation of the First and Second Commandments. Zephaniah, a distant relative of the royal family, had studied the Law and the earlier prophesies of Amos and Isaiah. He knew that all this wrong-doing would eventually be punished.

Zephaniah warned the people, and his preaching was later written down as a prophesy against the sins of worshipping other gods, of disobeying God's Laws, and of following pagan ways. His vision was of the coming "Day of the Lord" when God would search the hearts of all men. He would bless those that were faithful, punish the wicked, the idol-worshippers, and prove that their false gods were worthless.

HAGGAI AND ZECHARIAH

After their long captivity in distant Babylon, the Israelites were allowed to return to the ruined city of Jerusalem. God's great Temple had been burned down, and the people who lived in the city and the country nearby did not prosper. They had built themselves houses, planted crops and vineyards, but the harvests were poor and their spirits were depressed.

At this time two prophets arose, first Haggai and then Zechariah. They both saw these conditions and realized that the people were thinking only of themselves and not of their duty to God—which was to rebuild His temple and restore His worship. Zerubbabel, the governor, and Joshua, the high priest, listened to Haggai's message from God. They gathered the people together to bring wood, stone and other building materials so that they could once more build a Temple worthy of the Lord. They knew that by losing their indifference and going about this great work, the people would once again be blessed.

When the Temple was finished, God was pleased with the people's work. Although it was not as rich in treasures as the one that Solomon had built, it was filled with the people's spirit and love. Because of this, it was truly God's House and the center of people's lives.

Zechariah received God's messages in the form of visions, which were explained to him by angels. While Haggai saw chiefly the need for the re-building of the Temple, Zechariah saw the wider results of re-establishing God's rule in the world. One such vision was that of a man with a measuring line in his hand. When Zechariah asked the man where he was going, he replied that he was going to measure Jerusalem for a

wall, to see how long and wide it should be. And the man went on his
way. An angel of God stopped Zechariah and told him to run after the
man with the measuring line and say to him, "Jerusalem shall be without
walls, for her people shall multiply and spread all over the earth." God
Himself would be the wall and protector, for this was to be the new
Jerusalem, the city of God that included all the people of God everywhere.

MALACHI

The message of Malachi is found at the end of that portion of our Bible which is called the Old Testament. Like a library, the Bible is a collection of many books — some of history, some of poetry, some of law, and many dealing with wisdom, understanding, and knowledge of God. The words of those who spoke for God, the Prophets, were written down on long rolls of parchment, and these scrolls, as they are called, were carefully copied and preserved from one generation to another, down through the centuries. Thus there developed the written "Word of God" which men could study and teach. And while there would always be future prophets and preachers to bring the knowledge of God to His people, the Great Age of Hebrew prophesy was complete.

Malachi was not chiefly concerned with preaching against evil and injustice as were the earlier prophets, but with a better and clearer understanding of God and the way in which He was to be served and worshipped. Malachi knew that people would always have hard times and would become discouraged, and he told them that there is a divine purpose in all things and that in the end God's Will will be done. God's love for His people has been proved by the things He has done for them in the past. Since we were all created by the One God, we should treat all men as our brothers.

126

the new testament

THE NATIVITY

Joseph was a carpenter in Nazareth, a small town in the land of Israel. He was betrothed to marry Mary, who also lived in Nazareth. Shortly before his marriage Joseph had a strange dream. In it he saw an angel of the Lord, who came down from the heavens and spoke to Joseph.

The angel told him that after his marriage, Mary would have a son, sent by the Lord to save His people from their sins. And the angel said that the child should be called Jesus.

Now in those days, Israel was part of the Roman Empire, ruled over by the Emperor Caesar Augustus. Soon after Joseph and Mary were married, the Roman Emperor commanded all the citizens of the Empire to return to their own towns so that their names could be listed in a census. This would show how many people lived in the Empire, under Roman rule.

Both Joseph and Mary were descended from the Family of King David, so they returned to their home town of Bethlehem, King David's birthplace. When they reached Bethlehem, the town was filled with people who had come in from the countryside, to be listed by the Romans. Even though Mary was about to give birth, they could find no place to stay in Bethlehem. Finally they found lodging in a stable, where cattle were kept.

And there the baby was born. They had no crib for Him, so He was laid upon hay in a manger, which is the trough from which the cattle eat.

On the night of the baby's birth some shepherds were tending their sheep in the field near Bethlehem. Suddenly a great light shone upon them, and an angel of the Lord appeared. They were frightened by the vision, but the angel said to them:

"Be not afraid; for behold I bring you news of great joy, which shall be to all people; for there is born to you this day in Bethlehem, the city of David, a Saviour who is Christ the Lord." Then the angel told them how to find the child: "You will find a babe wrapped in swaddling clothes and lying in a manger."

Then they saw that the sky was filled with angels, and heard them singing: "Glory to God in the Highest. And on earth peace, good will toward men." Then the angels disappeared.

The shepherds immediately set out for the town. When they found Mary and Joseph with the babe lying in a manger, they repeated the message they had heard. Everyone was amazed. Mary, who had also been told by God of the great mission of her son, said nothing. But she thought deeply about these strange and wonderful happenings.

THE WISE MEN COME

After Jesus was born, Joseph and Mary stayed on in Bethlehem, for they did not want to travel with the newborn baby. One night, soon after the birth, three strangers appeared in the little town. They were richly dressed and it was clear they did not come from anywhere near Judea.

They had come from a land far to the east. They were men of great learning and wisdom, and had spent many years studying the stars and the mysteries of the world. One night they had seen a new and magnificent star shining in the sky. They knew what it meant—that a great king was born in the world and that the star would lead them to the newborn king.

The Wise Men decided to follow the star, so they might see this king and learn what He meant to the world. Their journey was long and hard. At last they came to the land of Judea. Thinking that everyone in the land would know of the new king, they asked, "Where is He that is born the king of the Jews? In the east we have seen His star; and we have come to worship Him." But no one they met had heard anything about a new king; they knew only that Herod still ruled the land under the Roman governor.

Word came to Herod that these three impressive visitors were asking about a new king. He was worried, for he knew that he was not popular with his people. He called the priests and scribes, the men who studied and taught the things that were predicted in the Bible, and asked them what the prophets had predicted about a new king coming to Israel. They told Herod that it was predicted that "out of Bethlehem in the land of Judah shall come forth one who shall rule my people."

Herod was frightened. He called for the three Wise Men and told them to find the child, so that he might also come and worship Him. But, of course, Herod was lying; he wanted to find the baby in order to destroy Him.

The Wise Men set out, and soon found the star again, shining high in the heavens above the road to Bethlehem. They followed it to the stable where Jesus was born. When they saw the child they knew at once that this was the one they had sought. They knelt before Him and presented gifts of gold and of rare perfumes called frankincense and myrrh, which were used at that time in religious ceremonies.

That same night, God warned the Wise Men in a dream not to return to Herod but to go back to their own land by a different road. Thus Herod did not find out where Jesus was.

The coming of Christ had long been predicted among the Jews, but they believed He would be the Saviour only of His own nation. The three Wise Men were the first men outside of Israel to know that Jesus had come for all men, and they were the first to see Him.

THE PRESENTATION
AT THE TEMPLE

It was a rule among the Jews that the first boy child born to a family was to be taken to the Temple in Jerusalem. There his parents would make an offering to the Lord, to show that the child belonged to the Lord.

When Jesus was forty days old, Joseph and Mary brought Him to the Temple. As an offering Joseph brought a pair of young pigeons to place upon the altar of the Temple.

Living in Jerusalem at that time was a very holy man, a man whom the Lord had spoken to directly. His name was Simeon, and he was very old, but the Lord had told him that he would not die until he had seen the Christ, or Saviour, whose coming had been predicted in the Bible.

One day the Spirit of the Lord urged Simeon to go to the Temple. He went, and was there when Joseph and Mary came with the baby Jesus, to present their offering. When Simeon saw the child, the Lord let him know that this was the Christ who had been promised.

Simeon took Jesus in his arms and gave thanks to the Lord for letting him see the Christ:

"Lord, now lettest thy servant depart in peace, according to thy word:
For mine eyes have seen thy salvation,
Which thou hast prepared before the face of all people;
A light to lighten the Gentiles,
And the glory of thy people Israel."

Then Simeon blessed Joseph and Mary. He also told Mary some of the things the future would hold, for her son and for her. He told her of the greatness her son would attain, but he added that sorrow, like a sword, would pierce her heart.

There was also in the Temple a woman named Anna, who spoke with God. She spent all her time praying. And the Lord also revealed to her that the baby Jesus was the Saviour who had been promised. She too gave thanks to the Lord, and told the other people in the Temple that the Redeemer had come.

And so it was that a few people who kept close to God knew Jesus was the Son of God. But to the rest of the people He was merely the son of a carpenter named Joseph, who came from Nazareth.

However, there was one other man in Israel who believed that Jesus was no ordinary child. This was the cruel King Herod. When Herod learned that the three Wise Men had returned home, without bringing him word of the child they called a king, he was furious. In his anger and fear he did a terrible thing. He gave orders to have all the children in Bethlehem, of two years old and under, killed. By doing this he felt sure he would eliminate the Christ child.

But God had already warned Joseph of Herod's cruel plans. So Joseph took Mary and the infant, and fled into Egypt, where Herod had no power. It was there the family stayed until King Herod died.

After Herod's death, Joseph set out to return to Bethlehem. But upon learning that Herod's cruel son Archelaus ruled that part of Israel, Joseph decided to go back to Nazareth, where he and Mary had grown up.

There, in the land of Galilee, Jesus grew to manhood, working with His father as a carpenter.

THE BOY JESUS
AND THE TEACHERS

The family of Jesus was very devoted in observing the religious ceremonies of their people. In those times, as today, a most important festival of the Jews was the Passover. This is the time when thanks are given to God for leading the Jews out of Egypt, where they had lived in bondage as slaves.

Every year Mary and Joseph travelled all the way from Nazareth to Jerusalem, the capital city, to celebrate the Passover in the Temple. Most people made the trip together, in groups, for travel in those days was hard and dangerous.

At the end of the Passover, the large caravan of friends and relatives set out to return to Nazareth. Jesus was by this time a strong, capable boy, unusually thoughtful, so His parents did not watch over Him all the time. He did not always travel with them, but often walked with friends or relatives in the caravan.

Joseph and Mary thought nothing of it when they did not see Him during the first day on the road. But when the caravan stopped for the night and Jesus did not appear for supper, they searched the camp for Him. When they discovered no one had seen Him that day, they returned to Jerusalem as fast as they could.

For three days the worried parents went about the city, looking for their son. Finally they found Him.

He was sitting in the Temple, surrounded by the wisest teachers and scholars in the country. And they were discussing the most serious ideas of religion with the twelve year old boy. When these learned men heard the answers Jesus gave to their difficult questions, they were astonished at the boy's knowledge and understanding.

Joseph and Mary were also astonished, when they saw their twelve year old son surrounded by learned men, and holding their interest. Mary was upset, as any mother would be. She told Jesus how anxious they had been, looking for Him, and she asked Him why He had caused them such worry.

Jesus seemed surprised that they did not know where He was.

"Did you not know that I would be in my Father's house?" He asked.

His parents did not really understand what He meant, although Mary knew deep down in her heart that Jesus would have to leave them one day, to carry out God's plan. And she and Joseph realized, that day in the Temple, that this was no mere boyish disobedience.

Jesus went back with His parents, and did everything they asked of Him, without question. And he remained with them in Nazareth, working as a carpenter with Joseph.

THE BAPTISM

Among the Hebrews in those days there appeared from time to time men who were known as prophets. They talked to the people as if they were speaking directly for God.

When Jesus was about thirty years old, a prophet named John was preaching to the people to give up their evil ways, because God was soon to appear on earth. When people came to him to repent their sins and promised to live a better life, John baptized them with water to show that bad things were washed away. They were made clean and ready for a better life. Thus he was known as John the Baptist; that is, the one who baptizes.

John was related to Jesus and their mothers had known each other many years before. But John and Jesus had never met, for John had spent most of his life in the wilds of the desert, seeking to learn about God. He dressed as a man of the wilderness in rough clothes of camel's hair and leather.

Many people came to be baptized by John in the River Jordan. Jesus heard of John and He travelled to the Jordan and asked John to baptize Him. When John saw Jesus he knew that here was the Son of God. He realized that standing before him was the very one he had preached would appear among them.

John did not feel he could baptize Jesus. He did not think he was worthy even to carry Jesus' shoes. John asked Jesus to baptize

him instead. But Jesus replied that it was proper for John to baptize Him. John knew that this was the greatest day of his life. It was the moment for which he had prayed, all those years in the wilderness, when he strived to learn what God wanted him to do. This was the day he had been preparing himself for.

So John baptized Jesus, and when Jesus came out of the water a wonderful thing happened. The sky seemed to split apart and a beautiful dove came down and settled on Jesus. At this moment the people heard a voice from heaven. The voice said: "This is my beloved Son, in whom I am well pleased."

THE TEMPTATION

Jesus was about thirty years old when He was baptized. Before then no one knew Him as anything more than a carpenter. The Bible tells us nothing of His life from the time when He was twelve and spoke with the wise men in the Temple, until the time He came to John to be baptized. But we know that He was being prepared to do God's work, to reveal the love of God to men.

But before He was to begin teaching, He had to go through one final intensive period of preparation. After His baptism, the spirit of God directed Jesus to go into the desert and live there alone: to pray and to think through how He would carry His message to all men.

So deep and serious was His concentration in that bare and lonely land, that He took no thought of eating or drinking. And for forty days He had no food or drink. But though He was the Son of God, Jesus was also a man of flesh and blood. When he had completed His preparation and was ready to return to the world, He realized that He was weak with hunger. Thus it was that when Jesus was at His weakest and his desires, such as hunger and thirst, were the strongest, He was tempted by evil.

After forty days in the desert without food, the spirit of evil, Satan, came to Jesus to test the strength of His spirit. First Satan said:

If you are the Son of God why don't you turn these stones into bread so that you can eat?

Jesus knew that all things were possible to God, but He knew that His power was given to Him not to help Himself, but only for others. He said to the evil spirit: "It is written, man shall not live by bread alone, but by every word of God".

Then the evil spirit led Jesus to Jerusalem, the holy city, and placed Him on a high tower of the Temple. There he urged Jesus to show the people that He was the Son of God by throwing Himself from the tower. "For", as Satan pointed out to Jesus, "it is written in the Bible that God shall give his angels charge of you and in their hands they will bear you up, lest you strike your foot against a stone."

But Jesus knew this would be wrong, for it would be done not to please God, but to show Himself before men and test the power of God when He had not been commanded by God to do this. He answered Satan: "It is written, 'you shall not tempt the Lord your God.'" That is, one must not do anything simply to test the power of God.

Then Satan tried to appeal to Jesus by the promise of power in the world. He took Jesus to a very high mountain and caused to appear to Him a vision of all the kingdoms of the world and all the glory that the ruler of the world could have. He offered to make Jesus King of all the world, saying, "All these I will give you, if you will fall down and worship me."

Jesus had heard enough. His spirit had not been weakened by all the temptations Satan could show Him. "Begone Satan!," Jesus said, "for it is written, 'You shall worship the Lord your God and him only shall you serve.'"

When Satan found that Jesus would not listen to him, he left. Then angels came from God and gave Jesus food and drink and all that He needed.

Satan would seem to have been beaten, but the Bible does not say that he went away forever; it tells us he departed to wait for another time to tempt Jesus.

THE CALLING OF THE DISCIPLES

When Jesus came out of the desert after His forty days of talking with God and after His turning away the temptations of evil, He was ready to bring His message to men. He did not gather crowds around him and begin teaching. He began with personal conversations with a few men who became interested in Him.

One day as Jesus walked near the River Jordan, where John the Baptist was teaching, John saw Him pass and said, "Behold, the Lamb of God." Two of the men standing there realized that John meant this was the Christ whose coming John had preached.

The two young men started up the path after Jesus. Jesus saw them coming and stopped and asked them, "What is it that you seek?" They asked where Jesus was staying so they might come and talk with Him. And Jesus replied, "Come and see."

So the men went with Jesus. They were fishermen from the Sea of Galilee who had come to hear John the Baptist teach. One of them was called Andrew.

Andrew spent the entire day talking with Jesus and learning from Him. He went away from this meeting certain that he had met the Son of God and the King of Israel. All the Jews of that time, even simple fishermen like Andrew, knew that the Bible foretold there would come a man of God—a man who would save their people from sin and restore them to union with God. They believed, too, that He would be king of their nation.

Andrew brought his brother Simon to meet Jesus. Jesus saw him coming and without waiting to be introduced to him said, "So you are Simon, son of Jona?" Then Jesus gave him a new name. "You shall be called 'the Rock,'" he told Simon. So from that time Simon was called Simon Peter, or Simon the Rock.

The next day Jesus decided to go to Galilee. On the way he met another Galilean named Philip. Jesus said, "Follow me." Such was the sense of power in Jesus that Philip immediately joined him. Philip had a friend, Nathanael, who came from a town not far from Nazareth, where Jesus had grown up. When Philip told Nathanael about Jesus, Nathanael, who did not think much of Nazareth, remarked, "Can anything good come out of Nazareth?" Philip did not argue with him. "Come and see," he said, knowing only that Jesus could convince Nathanael.

When Jesus saw Nathanael approaching he remarked, "Here is an Israelite indeed, in whom there is no guile."

Nathanael was surprised. "How did you know me?" he asked.

"Before Philip called you," Jesus replied, "when you were under the fig tree, I saw you."

Nathanael did not understand how Jesus could have seen him when he was miles away. Immediately he believed what Philip had told him of Jesus. "Teacher," he said, "you are the Son of God! You are the King of Israel!"

Jesus gently reproved him. "Because I said to you I saw you under the fig tree, do you believe? You shall see greater things than these. You will see heaven opened and the angels of God ascending and descending upon the Son of Man."

Later Jesus found John with his brother James mending their nets in their boat with Zebedee, their father. He called them, and they left their father in the boat with the hired servants and followed Him.

Jesus now had six followers travelling with Him. Andrew and Simon Peter, who were brothers; John and James, who were brothers; and Philip and Nathanael. These men are called Disciples, which means students.

THE REJECTION
AT NAZARETH

Jesus wanted to bring His message of God's love first to His own people in Nazareth. He had always attended the synagogue, and when He returned He went to worship with His fellow townspeople there on the Sabbath.

The news of the wonderful works He had done had spread through the town. The Temple was crowded with people who had known Jesus as a simple carpenter, and they wondered what He might be like, now that He was said to be a prophet and a miracle worker.

Jesus stood up, as was the custom, to show that He wanted to read from the Bible. He was handed the book of the prophet Esaias. He opened the book, and found the place where it was written:

"The spirit of the Lord *is* upon me,

Because he has annointed me to preach good news to the poor.

He has sent me to proclaim release to the captives,

And recovering of sight to the blind,

To set at liberty those who are oppressed,

To proclaim the acceptable year of the Lord."

He closed the book, returned it to the attendant, and sat down. The eyes of the congregation were fixed on Him. Jesus spoke:

"Today this scripture has been fulfilled in your hearing."

The people were astonished. This was a serious and great claim, almost frightening. That these words of the Holy Bible applied to Him, Jesus; that the inspired prophet Isaiah had been writing about the simple carpenter of Nazareth!

"Where did this man get this wisdom and these mighty words?" they muttered. "Is not this the carpenter's son, a carpenter Himself? Is not His mother called Mary? Are not His brothers James and Joseph and Simon and Judas? And are not all His sisters with us? Where than did *this man* get all this?"

Jesus realized that they could not understand that He who had lived among them could be the Son of God. He told them: "Truly I say to you, no prophet is accepted in his own country." And he told two stories from the Bible to make the point clear to them. Both were stories of prophets who had made miracles. His point was that in both cases the Lord had sent the prophets not to their own people, but to outsiders, for their own people would not have accepted them.

This made the people in the synagogue very angry. They may have felt that Jesus was saying they were not as good as the people of other towns. Certainly they were sure He had no right to claim to fulfill the prophecy of the Bible.

The people seized Him and led Him out of the city to the top of a high and dangerous cliff, preparing to push him over the cliff. Somehow His calm, fearless manner was such that no one wanted to make the first move. He walked quietly through the crowd and down the road, leaving them standing in confusion. No one wanted to pursue Him.

Sadly Jesus went down from the hills to the city of Capernaum, on the shore of the Sea of Galilee, and there He taught in the synagogues, and the people listened.

THE WOMAN AT THE WELL

John the Baptist continued to preach and to baptize followers after Jesus had begun to become widely known through the country. As Jesus gained more followers, John had less, but he continued to preach that Jesus was the Christ, while he was no more than "the voice of one crying in the wilderness" to prepare people for the message of Jesus.

John was a fearless preacher who condemned sins wherever he found them, no matter how powerful the sinners might be. He even preached against King Herod (the son of the Herod who was king when Christ was born). He attacked the sins of Herod's wife Herodias and she demanded that Herod have John killed. Herod feared the truth that John spoke and refused to kill him. But to satisfy his wife and perhaps to protect John from her hatred, he had John imprisoned.

Jesus had been teaching in and around Jerusalem in Judea. When he heard that John had been imprisoned in Galilee, He set out for that country. Between Judea and Galilee, in the mountains, there was a country called Samaria and the people living there were known as Samaritans.

The people of Galilee, Judea and the other places where Christ preached were Jews, but the Samaritans were not part of the nation of Israel. They were related to the Jews, and they worshipped the same God. But they had different forms of worship and their Bible had only the first five books of the Old Testament. They did not regard the prophets as speaking for God.

Because of these differences, there had grown up much bad feeling between the Samaritans and Jews. Most Jews travelling from Judea to Galilee usually went way out of their way to avoid passing through Samaria. But Jesus struck out straight across the mountains of Samaria.

One morning during this trip Jesus stopped, very tired, beside a famous old well. This well had been dug by Jacob, the ancestor of all the Israelites centuries before, and was called Jacob's well.

Jesus was thirsty, as well as hungry and tired, but he couldn't get water from the well without a jar and a rope to pull it up. His Disciples had gone into the nearby village of Sychar to buy food. As He waited, a Samaritan woman came to the well with her jar to draw water. Jesus asked her for a drink.

She could tell from His dress and speech that Jesus was a Jew. "How is it," she asked surprised, "that you a Jew ask a drink of me, a woman of Samaria? Jews have no dealings with Samaritans."

Jesus answered her. "If you knew the gift of God and who it is that is saying to you, 'Give me a drink,' you would have asked him, and he would have given you living water."

The woman said, "Sir, you have nothing to draw with and the well is deep. Where do you get that living water? Are you greater than our father Jacob, who gave us this well, and drank from it himself, and his sons, and his cattle?"

Jesus said to her, "Everyone who drinks of this water will thirst again, but whoever drinks of the water that I shall give him, will never thirst; the water that I shall give him will become in him a well of water springing up into everlasting life."

The woman said to him, "Sir, give me this water, that I may not thirst, nor come here to draw."

Then Jesus told the woman of things she had done in her life, which no stranger could have known. The woman was deeply impressed and felt this man must have powers known only to God. She asked him whether the Samaritans were right in worshipping God on the mountain as their fathers had done, or whether the Jews were right and that Jerusalem was the place where men should go to worship God.

Jesus replied: "Woman, believe me, the hour is coming when ye shall neither on this mountain, nor in Jerusalem worship the Father. The hour is coming, and is now here, when true worshippers will worship the Father in spirit and truth . . . God is spirit and those who worship Him must worship Him in spirit and truth."

And the woman understood that Jesus was saying that a temple was not necessary to worship God, and that He could be worshipped anywhere by those who love His spirit and understand His truth.

The woman at the well then said to Jesus: "I know that a Messiah is coming, He who is called Christ, and when He comes He will show us all things."

And Jesus said "I that speak to you am he."

It was then that the Disciples returned from the town with food, and the woman left her water jug, and went into the town. She told

the people: "Come see a man who told me all that I ever did. Can this be the Christ?"

And the people left the town, and went to see Jesus, at the well.

Meanwhile the Disciples offered Jesus the food they had brought. But Jesus had forgotten about food. "My food," He told them, "is to do the will of Him who sent me, and to finish His work."

The Samaritans were so impressed with the woman's words that when they found Jesus at the well they asked him to stay and teach them about God. He stayed for two days, and many more believed in Him when they heard His words.

TRAVELLING AND TEACHING

So far as we know from the Bible, Jesus spent most of His life in the little town of Nazareth, working quietly as a carpenter with His earthly father Joseph.

He was in full manhood when He travelled from His native village to be baptized by John the Baptist, and only three years elapsed from that time until His death. During this brief time all His great teaching was accomplished. In those few years during His thirties, He spoke the words that much of the world, two thousand years later, still seeks to live by.

Though His message was for all the world, during His lifetime Jesus spoke mostly to His own people. He never preached in any of the great Roman cities, which were the centers of power in His time. He travelled almost continually throughout the lands where the people of the Old Testament had spread—lands that we now call simply The Holy Land.

Many times He crossed the great inland seas, such as the Sea of Galilee, by boat; and He may have ridden donkeys or camels from time to time. But mostly He and His Disciples walked. Along hot and dusty roads, over rugged mountains, they walked with little thought of where they were to sleep or what they were to eat.

Most of the teaching was in small towns, and in some of these, such as Capernaum, Jesus spent a good deal of time. And when He returned to His own village of Nazareth He was rejected by His former neighbors.

He journeyed to Jerusalem for the Passover celebrations three times during His ministry.

Though He travelled extensively, Jesus did not seek out people to teach. Frequently, He retired to the mountains or the desert to be alone with God, or confined His teaching to His Disciples. But wherever He went among people, *they* sought Him out. His fame spread from Galilee, where He called His first Disciples and began His teaching, throughout all the Roman province of Syria, which included the Jewish kingdoms.

Romans and other outsiders in this area knew of Him, and some came to believe in Him during His life. And yet it was not until He had been rejected by His own people that the world beyond the Holy Land came to know of Jesus and His message from God.

CANA'S WEDDING FEAST

When Jesus went out to teach in the world, He did not forget His family and His friends. He lived a simple and rugged life, spending long sojourns alone in the desert. But unlike John the Baptist He was not a lonely hermit.

After He returned from His trips in the mountains or desert, He went out among the people. For He knew He must teach His message to all mankind. All kinds of people liked to be with Him, for because of His great love for all men He was a wise counsellor and warm friend.

And we know from His first miracles that He wanted those around Him to be happy. During the time of His great teaching, Jesus performed many miracles. All of them were meant to awaken people to the great truth He was bringing from God. For Jesus felt that by performing a miracle, an act made possible only by God's divine will, He could show the world God's great authority over the Universe.

But sometimes Jesus seemed unwilling to perform miracles. He did them only when He needed to show God's power, and when someone needed help. Of course the people were impressed by His miracles, and talked of them to others. And many who came *only* to see the miracles, heard the message of Jesus and through Him came to know God.

Shortly after Jesus met His first followers He was invited to a wedding in the town of Cana near His home in Nazareth. In those times, as today, a feast always followed the wedding, and Jesus attended it with His mother, Mary.

Before the feast was over, all the wine had been used and there was none left for the guests. Jesus' mother knew that He had the power to do anything, and she said to Him: "They have no wine."

Jesus tried to explain to His mother that it was not yet time for Him to show the power of God in Him by performing miracles. But Mary knew that Jesus would help His friends, and provide wine for them so that the feast could continue. So she said to the servants: "Do whatever He tells you."

Six stone jars were standing nearby, each holding twenty or thirty gallons.

Jesus told the servants: "Fill the jars with water." They filled them, and Jesus then said: "Now draw some of the water out of the jars, and take it to the steward."

The servants were amazed when they saw that the water they had placed in the jars had turned to wine. But they did as Jesus said, and took the wine to the steward. When the steward (the man hired to run the wedding feast) tasted the wine he, too, was amazed. And he told the bridegroom: "Every man serves the good wine first; and when men have drunk freely, then the poor wine. But you have kept the good wine until now."

THE GREAT CATCH OF FISH

Four of Jesus' first followers were fishermen. They were the brothers Andrew and John, and two other brothers, Philip and Peter. These men fished in the Sea of Galilee, a huge inland lake.

In the land around the Sea of Galilee Jesus had attracted many who wanted to hear His message. He was especially popular in the town of Capernaum. One day when He was staying there he went out to the

160

lake. He was followed by a great crowd of people who had been eagerly waiting to hear Him speak and perhaps hoping they would see a miracle. On the shores of the lake were two boats, one of which belonged to Simon Peter and Andrew. The other was operated by the brothers James and John and their father Zebedee. The fishermen were working on their nets on the shore.

Jesus wanted all in the crowd to see and hear Him, so he stepped into the boat of Simon Peter and his brother Andrew. He asked them to push it out into the middle of the lake, so the crowd gathered on the shore would not be pressed around him. The fishermen sent the boat into the lake and Jesus spoke to the people from the boat, as they stood on the beach.

When Jesus had spoken, and the people had gone, He saw that the fishermen had not caught any fish on their last trip. He told Simon Peter to take the boat out into the deep water and let down his nets for fish. Simon Peter replied that they had fished all night without catching anything. But he knew that whatever Jesus told him to do would be the right thing, so they rowed toward the middle of the lake.

They put out their nets and soon felt the powerful tug of fish in them. They tried to pull in the net and found that it was so full they could not. They called to James and John in their boat nearby to help. The four men hauling with all their might finally got the net up to the boat and shoals of fish came pouring into it. There were so many fish that both boats almost sank.

This was a catch such as they had never seen from the lake.

Simon Peter was overcome with amazement at the sight. He realized that Jesus had powers he could not understand. He fell at the feet of Jesus said said: "Depart from me, for I am a sinful man, O Lord." Peter felt that he did not deserve such a gift from God, and could not walk with the Son of God. But Jesus said to him: "Do not be afraid. Henceforth you will be fishers of men."

And Simon Peter understood that Jesus meant he should leave his fishing and join Him in helping to spread His word to other men.

When they got back to the land, all four fisherman abandoned their nets and their boats. They went with Jesus, to learn from Him, and to help Him teach others.

On the following Sabbath they went with Jesus to the synagogue, and Jesus spoke to the people and tried to teach them. But the people were surprised at His teachings, for the scribes in the synagogue taught only what had been written before, while Jesus taught as one who spoke directly for God. He did not need the support of words others had written.

JESUS CALMS THE STORM

When large crowds of people came to hear Jesus speak, He could always tell how much the people who were listening to Him could understand. He knew that many came *not* to learn, but hoping to see a great miracle performed. And he always knew when to send them away, or to leave them.

One day He had been teaching by the Sea of Galilee, when He decided it was time to leave the crowds. So He got into a boat and asked His Disciples to head for the other side of the sea. Jesus took the opportunity of the long boat trip to rest. He lay down in the stern of the boat and fell asleep.

Suddenly the sky darkened, and a wind began to blow. It grew so fierce that great waves rose in the lake, rocking the little boat. As the storm grew worse, even the hardened fishermen were frightened. They felt sure the boat would be destroyed. Terrified they awakened Jesus, and shouted to Him over the howling wind: "Master, don't you care if we are all drowned?"

Jesus looked at the raging sea. Then calmly He said to the waves: "Peace . . . be still."

162

The wind suddenly stopped blowing, the sea flattened out, and the boat lay still on the calm water. He turned to His Disciples and asked them: "Why are you afraid? Have you no faith?"

The fishermen looked at each other and said: "Who then is this, that even the wind and sea obey Him?"

Many times Jesus did such things before His Disciples—not to demonstrate power, but to teach them that they must not worry about themselves, but rather believe and trust in God.

THE FEEDING OF THE MULTITUDE

Jesus had sent His followers out to preach in His name in the villages surrounding the Sea of Galilee. And when they returned, they were followed by thousands who had heard the message. The multitudes had come to seek Jesus out, to hear Him teach and to be healed of sickness.

Jesus often wanted to escape from the crowds, to have time to teach His Disciples. One day He and His Disciples got into a boat and set out for a lonely spot where they could be together undisturbed, eat a little, rest and talk. But those who saw them leave called to the others, and a great crowd ran around the lake. They got to the other side ahead of the boat carrying Jesus and His followers.

Jesus took pity on the people who were so eager to be with Him, so He taught them and healed those who were sick and asked for His help. They were faraway from the village, and Jesus had not eaten all day. Neither had the great multitudes who had followed Him. One of the Disciples' suggested Jesus should send the people back to their homes to eat.

But Jesus replied: "You give them something to eat."

And the Disciple asked: "Shall we go back to the village and buy bread for the crowds, so that they can eat?"

Jesus said: "How many loaves and fishes do you have?"

The Disciple looked, and found only a little food. He said: "Five loaves and two fishes."

Jesus turned to the crowd, and told them to sit down on the grass in groups of fifties and hundreds. Then taking the five loaves and two fishes. He looked up to heaven and blessed the food. Then He broke the loaves and gave them to the Disciples to set before the people: and He divided the fishes among them all.

Everyone in the great crowd ate and were satisfied. Indeed they could not even finish all the food. There were twelve baskets of bread and fish left over.

Thus from the five loaves and the two fishes five thousand people had been fed.

JESUS WALKS ON THE WATER

After the thousands who had followed Jesus across the lake had been fed from the five loaves and two fishes, Jesus sent them away, though they were ready to proclaim Him as their king.

He also told His Disciples to get in the boat and go back across the lake without Him. They did not want to leave Him, but they obeyed.

Jesus then went up into the hills beyond the lake to pray alone. As the Disciples were crossing the lake a strong wind blew up and they had to row very hard to keep from being blown back to the shore where they had started.

Then one of them looked up from his oar and pointed out across the water. There was a ghostly figure walking past their boat, walking on the water as if it were dry land. They were terrified and they cried out.

But it was Jesus, and He spoke to them. "Take heart," He said, "It is I; have no fear."

Then Peter spoke up and said, "Lord, if it be you, let me come to you walking on the water." Jesus told him to get out of the boat and walk toward Him. Peter found that he too was walking upon the water. Suddenly he was afraid. He forgot his faith in Jesus and immediately he began to sink. He cried out, "Lord, save me!"

Jesus reached out His hand and caught hold of Peter, lifting him up. "Oh man of little faith," He said to Peter, "why did you doubt me?"

Jesus took Peter back to the boat and got into it with the Disciples. Immediately the wind stopped blowing and they rowed on across the lake.

When they got to the other side, the people recognized Jesus and brought the sick for him to heal. Everywhere He went, sick people were brought to Him and those who even touched the hem of his garment and believed were made well.

The people had not forgotten the feeding of the five thousand from the few loaves and fishes and many sought Jesus out hoping the miracle would be repeated. But He explained to them that they must not seek merely for bread, "but for the food which endures to eternal life, which the Son of Man will give to you. . . ."

THE CASTING OUT
OF THE MONEY CHANGERS

Jesus was faithful to the religious observances of His people. He attended all the ceremonies that marked the great events of the Jewish nation. An important day is the Feast of the Passover. This celebrates the freeing of the Jews from their slavery in Egypt. Every year all who were able traveled to the Temple in Jerusalem for this feast.

Not long after Jesus had called His first Disciples and shortly after He had done the miracle of changing water to wine, He traveled to Jerusalem for the Passover.

It was the practice for the people to offer gifts of sheep and cattle and doves upon the altar as a recognition that they were God's children. Since many traveled from far away they did not bring the animals with them, but bought them in Jerusalem. Those who sold the animals for the sacrifices, and those who changed the money of the travelers had come to set up their shops within the Temple itself. The Temple looked more like a market place than a place to worship God.

When Jesus saw this He decided to rid the Temple of the money changers and the sellers of animals. He took some rope and made a whip of it. Swinging this whip he moved among the buyers and sellers. There were many of them and He was but a single man, but the sense of power and truth in Jesus was so strong that the mob fled in panic. Jesus drove out all the animals and tipped over the money of the money changers. Then He said to them: "Take these things hence; make not my Father's house a place of buying and selling."

When those who watched had recovered from their surprise at this powerful stranger, they approached Him and asked Him what He could do that would show them the authority by which He had acted. Jesus replied, "Destroy this Temple and in three days I will raise it up." They pointed out to Him that it had taken forty-six years to build the Temple, and they did not understand how He could rear it up in three days. Jesus was talking of a time to come, when He would be killed. The Temple of His body would be destroyed, but in three days He would rise up.again. Later when Jesus was crucified, His Disciples remembered what He had said on this day, and understood what he meant.

While He was in Jerusalem, Jesus performed miracles that brought many people in the Capital to believe that He was indeed the Son of God.

THE FIRM FOUNDATION

When Jesus spoke to the people He did so in simple terms, so that they could easily understand Him. He talked of real things that they knew from their own daily activities, such as planting and reaping grain, tending sheep, or building a house.

At the end of His greatest sermon Jesus sought to impress His listeners with the choice before them—either heeding God's truth or ignoring it. And to illustrate it clearly to them, He told them the story of Rock and Sand.

"Therefore whosoever heareth these sayings of mine and doeth them," He said, "I will liken him unto a wise man who built his house upon a rock. And the rain descended and the floods came and the winds blew and beat upon that house. And it fell not; for it was founded upon a rock.

"And everyone that heareth these sayings of mine and doeth them not, shall be likened unto the foolish man, who built his house upon sand. And the rains descended and the floods came and the winds blew and beat upon that house. And it fell; and great was the fall of it."

And the people understood His simple illustration. For they knew that the rains can wash away sand and leave a house without foundations, that such a house must collapse. But the house built on rock cannot be washed away by the rains. The foundations stay strong, and the house weathers the flood.

The wisest in the crowds who listened to Jesus knew, then, that He meant that their lives must be built upon the rock of truth. For while it may be easier to build on sand, only the rock will stay firm when the storm of troubles comes. And we ourselves know that this is indeed true.

THE SOWER

The message Jesus brought to the world was so new and so different from anything people had known before that even His Disciples sometimes had trouble understanding Him. But Jesus wanted to reach not only the educated or wise, but everyone, including those who thought about little else but their day-to-day problems.

To move all people to think about God and the message of love He

brought from God, Jesus taught the people by means of stories which they could easily understand. These teaching stories are called parables.

The first parable that is reported in the Bible is about a farmer and is called the Parable of the Sower. In those days, some plants, such as wheat, were planted by sowing or scattering the seeds upon the ground.

Jesus told the people of a farmer who was sowing seed. As he sowed, some of the seeds fell beside the road where the ground was trampled down. People walking on the road stepped on the seed and destroyed the new plants. Some of the seed fell where the soil was thin because there were rocks under it. These seeds grew quickly, but late in the summer when the sun was hot, they dried up. There was not enough soil to hold the moisture for them. Some seeds fell where weeds were growing and these seeds could not get started. But some of the seeds fell into rich earth which the farmer had prepared. They grew and produced far more grains of wheat than had been planted as seed.

The Disciples were not sure of the meaning of this story. When they were alone with Jesus they asked Him. And He explained the Parable of the Sower to them, so that they could truly understand its meaning.

Jesus told His Disciples that in the parable He Himself was the sower, the one who spoke God's words. The seeds, He explained, were the words that he spoke.

The seeds that fell by the roadside were His words heard by people who did not really listen, and the truth was quickly taken away from them by the evil forces of life.

The seeds that fell on the shallow and rocky ground were His words as heard by those who responded to them with joy and excitement, but who had so little depth of thought and feeling they were soon distracted by other interests. The plants died before they bore grain.

The seeds that fell among the weeds and thorns were His words heard by those whose lives were too crowded by the little problems of living. They could not think about new ideas, and just went on worrying about their petty affairs.

But the seeds that fell on the fertile ground were His words heard by those who listen, who care, who take the truth into their hearts and keep it alive. Through them the seeds will bear beautiful grain.

THE LOST SHEEP

Jesus traveled far and wide throughout the land of Israel with his Disciples, touching every part of that ancient kingdom as He preached the word of God and ministered to the sick and needy. Always as he went, the word of His wondrous message of love and of His miraculous deeds went before Him. On every side He was met by great multitudes eager to see and hear this new prophet.

After Jesus had toured all the rest of the country, He turned His attention to Perea, that part of Israel east of the Jordan River, which He had not as yet visited. But before Jesus went Himself to Perea He sent seventy of His followers ahead of Him to prepare the people. He sent them out in pairs with the same commands, He had given the twelve Disciples when He sent them through Galilee.

He said, "I send you forth as lambs among the wolves. See that you carry no purse or bag for food and only the shoes that you are now wearing. Go only to the villages, preaching to the people and healing the sick. Tell them, 'The Kingdom of God is coming.'"

When all was prepared, Jesus went into the land of Perea to continue His ministry. The seventy chosen followers had spread the word of His coming to every village, and at each He was greeted by great throngs of people. But as always there were enemies of Jesus among the crowds, who did their best to discredit Him. These were mainly the Pharisees and Scribes who were overzealous in their strict adherence to the laws of the Jewish faith. Jesus' commonsense approach to the laws and the worship of God angered them, and they did everything they could to turn the people against Jesus.

The crowds that came to hear Jesus were composed of many kinds of people. There were farmers and fishermen, tradespeople, shepherds, publicans, the Pharisees and Scribes, and even Roman soldiers. Most of the people were good and faithful to their religion, but there were some the Pharisees called "sinners" who were not permitted to worship in the temple because of their misdeeds.

Jesus was concerned with both the good and the bad, and in one of the villages in Perea the Pharisees tried to use this against Him. These enemies of Jesus said to the people, "Look, this man likes to have sinners come to see Him, and He even eats with them."

Jesus answered with a parable that is called "The Lost Sheep."

"What man of you," he said, "who has one hundred sheep and one of them is lost, would not leave the other ninety-nine and go look for the one that is lost? And when he finds it says to his neighbors, 'Be glad with me; for I have found my sheep which was lost.'

"Even so," Jesus said, "there is joy in heaven over one sinner who has turned to God, more than over ninety and nine good men who do not need to turn from their sins."

The Pharisees and Scribes were unable to answer, and the people realized through this parable that Jesus came more to seek sinners and the needy of the world, than those who thought themselves too good to need His help.

THE GOOD SAMARITAN

On one occasion Jesus taught another lesson with one of His parables. As we know Jesus often answered questions with parables, those stories that taught truths in such ways that the listeners' belief in their own righteousness was often shaken.

One day a scribe, a man whose job was to copy and teach the Bible, asked Jesus, "Master, what shall I do to have everlasting life?" Jesus had been teaching the way to everlasting life and the scribe wished to test him.

Jesus replied, "What is written in the law? You are a reader of the Bible; tell me what it says."

The scribe, of course, was ready with the answer from the Old Testament. "You shall love the Lord your God with all your heart and with all your soul and with all your strength, and with all your mind; and you shall love your neighbor as yourself." The scribe had answered his own question, which was what Jesus had wanted him to do, but he was unsatisfied that Jesus had not engaged him in argument, so he asked, "And who is my neighbor?"

Jesus knew that to Jewish leaders such as this scribe, the most hated people were the Samaritans, a nation of people who shared many of the Jewish traditions, but had their own forms of worshipping God. To make His lesson particularly clear, Jesus told the scribe the parable of the Good Samaritan.

One day, said Jesus, a Jew, traveling the lonely road from Jerusalem to Jericho, was attacked by robbers, stripped of his clothes and beaten nearly to death. Shortly afterward a priest, a countryman of the victim's, passed by, and when he saw the wounded man, crossed the road and hurried away. Then another man of a priestly family, the Levites, came along, and he, too, scurried by on the other side of the road.

Then came along a Samaritan, a man who could hardly be expected to help in a land where he was hated; but the Samaritan stopped and treated the man's wounds, and put him on his own donkey and took him to an inn. There he left money for the man's care and told the innkeeper if more were needed, he would pay on his return trip.

Then Jesus asked the scribe, "Which of these three was neighbor to the man who had been attacked by the robbers?"

And the scribe, impressed by the story, answered, "He that showed mercy on him."

"Go then and do likewise," said Jesus.

Thus the scribe learned that a neighbor is not just one who lives nearby, but anyone in the world who has love in his heart—that all men of good will are neighbors.

THE UNJUST STEWARD

While traveling in Perea, Jesus told the people many of the parables which were later recorded in the New Testament. And while in Perea, Jesus again told His Disciples of what was to come to pass in Jerusalem in a few weeks time. He said that all that the prophets had said about the Son of God would come true in Jerusalem: that He would be made prisoner, mocked, spit upon and beaten and then killed. But on the third day, He told them, He would rise again. These words the Disciples found hard to understand or believe, but they could readily understand the simple truths of the parables he told. One of the last stories he told while traveling in Perea was the parable of the Unjust Steward.

There was a certain rich man, Jesus said, who had trusted the management of his estate to a steward. This was a common practice of the day, and the steward enjoyed almost complete authority in the handling of his master's business. But such freedom had led this steward into constant temptation to cheat his master, and one day he was discovered. The rich man sent for him and said, "What is this I hear about you? You shall soon give up your place and be my steward no more."

The steward became desperate when faced with the loss of his job and thought to himself, "What shall I do? In a few days I will lose my place and I am too weak to work in the fields and too ashamed to go begging from door to door." But he was a very clever man and figured out a scheme that would win him friends who would take care of him when he would have to leave. His plan was simple. He sent for the men who were in debt to his master and asked them, "How much do you owe my master?"

"I owe him a hundred measures of oil," the first debtor said.

The steward said to him, "Pay him only fifty measures. Then the steward tore up the old note and made this man a new one for the lesser amount.

To the other he said, "How much do you owe him?" And this one answered, a hundred measures of wheat."

The steward then tore up his note and made him a new one saying, "Pay him for only eighty measures."

When the rich man learned of how his unfaithful steward had further cheated him he marveled and said, "He is a clever thief and a skillful swindler and takes good care of himself."

Jesus, although he did not approve of the steward's action, told those listening that the master's admiration was not unfounded, and pointed out the lesson that many people will often work harder to preserve and increase their worldly gains than they will to safeguard their spiritual interests.

THE PRODIGAL SON

The people of Jesus' time and country had a great respect for justice. They felt that life must be lived by strict rules and that people should be rewarded or punished according to how closely they followed the rules of their society.

Jesus respected the laws and customs of His people, but He had a new message to bring to mankind, and it was not composed of rules on how to act. It was the joyful news that the love of God for every person has no limit. No matter how bad any person is, all of God's love is there for him if he will only give himself to God with all his heart. To bring this great truth home to his listeners Jesus seemed deliberately to try to upset their ordinary ideas of what was fair.

When Jesus was teaching in Perea, the last part of Israel He was to visit, he told the people the parable of the Prodigal Son. Prodigal means wasteful, and this son was wasteful. He asked his father for his share of wealth that he would inherit, and the father divided all that he had between his two sons.

The prodigal son, the younger of the two brothers, went off to a far country where he spent everything he had in wild and foolish living. Soon he was penniless, and then his sufferings began. There was a shortage of food in the country, and though he worked like a slave, he became so hungry that he tried to eat the food that he was supposed to feed to the animals.

Finally he decided to return to his father's house. He did not expect to be taken back as a son, but to work as a servant; he knew his father's servants had enough to eat.

As he approached the house his father ran out to meet him. The boy cried, "Father, I have sinned against heaven and before you and am no more worthy to be called your son." Nevertheless, his father ordered the servants to bring the boy the best of everything in his house. He ordered the finest meat prepared, which meant killing the fatted calf, the prize

of the herd. He ordered a great feast with music and dancing, saying, "Let us eat and be merry."

The other son, returning from a hard day's work, was angry when he learned what was going on and would not enter the house to greet his brother. He explained his anger to his father. "These many years I have served you," he said, "and have never disobeyed anything you ordered, yet you have never given me even a young goat to have a feast for my friends."

"Son," the father told him, "you are ever with me, and all I have is yours. It is proper that we should make merry now, for your brother was dead, and is alive again. He was lost, and is found."

With this story Jesus taught the people that He had come not for those who thought they were good, but for those who knew they had sinned.

THE CALLING OF MATTHEW

Tax collectors have never been popular. And among the Jews who were then ruled by the Romans, the publicans, as the tax collectors for the Romans were called, were the most despised men in the country. They were regarded as traitors to their people and sinners because they could not join in the religious life of the Jews.

One day, when Jesus was going toward the Sea of Galilee followed by a great crowd of people, He saw a publican sitting at his table collecting taxes from the people.

Jesus could know what a man was really like in his heart, even if He had never seen him before. When He saw the publican whose name was Matthew, he knew that this man would become one of His greatest followers. Jesus said simply, "Follow me."

Matthew rose and joined Jesus without a word or a question. The people could not understand how Jesus could have a hated publican among His Disciples, but Jesus knew that Matthew would one day write one of the great books of the Bible, The Gospel According to Matthew.

When Jesus went to Matthew's house, Matthew prepared a great feast to which He invited some publicans and others whom the leaders of the Jews considered sinners.

When the Pharisees saw this, they drew aside some of Jesus' Disciples and, hoping to raise discontent among them, said, "Why does your master eat with publicans and sinners?"

Jesus heard the question and replied to the Pharisees, "Those that are well do not need a doctor, but those that are sick do." He told them that He knew these people were sinners, but that He came not to save those who were good, or thought they were, but those who were sinners and wanted to be better.

THE WORKERS
IN THE VINEYARD

During his ministry Jesus often referred to the fact that the Jews would not be the chosen people in the Kingdom of God which He was bringing to the world, but that the Gentiles would be God's chosen people. This was a different interpretation of what the prophets of the Old Testament had said. Jesus explained it in the parable of the Workmen in the Vineyard.

A rich man had planted a vineyard, Jesus said, with a hedge and a ditch around the new field and a tall watch-tower in the middle of it. Then he let the vineyard out to a group of workmen to care for, while he went on a journey. The men tended the vineyard well and produced a bountiful crop. The master of the vineyard, returned from his trip, sent his servants to the workmen to collect his share of the grapes. But the workmen laid hold of the servants and beat one, killed another and stoned and drove away the third. The master then sent more of his servants to collect his share, but they too were driven off by the workmen.

Not knowing what to do next, the master finally decided to send his son to collect his share of the fruit from the workmen, saying, "They will surely respect my son." But the workmen, seeing the son coming, said among themselves, "Come, let us kill him, and we shall have his inheritance." The workmen seized the son, threw him out of the vineyard and slew him.

Then Jesus asked the people listening to Him, "When the master of the vineyard comes, what will he do to these workmen who slew his son?" And the people gathered about Jesus answered, "He will destroy those wretches and entrust his vineyard to other workmen who will render up unto him the fruits that are his."

And Jesus answered them, saying, "Have you never read the Scriptures? 'The stone which the builders rejected, the same is become the cornerstone; this is the Lord's doing and it is wonderful in our eyes.' Wherefore I say to you that the Kingdom of God shall be taken from you, and shall be given to a nation that will yield its fruits."

THE TRIBUTE MONEY

Jesus rose early one morning during his last days in Jerusalem and went to the Temple where a great multitude waited to hear Him. They had risen early, despite the cold of the day, to look again upon the person of this divine miracle worker and to listen to the message of hope and salvation He brought to them. His enemies had not stayed away, and the Pharisees and others who hated and feared Jesus were also present in the crowd. They were there in the hope that they might discredit this new prophet who had won the people's admiration.

Because of the cold, Jesus walked back and forth under the portico of the Temple as he preached to the people. During a pause in his message the Pharisees launched their attack on Jesus by posing a question which they thought would trap Him.

"Master," they said, "we know you are truthful and sincere and teach the way of God in truth, and that thou carest naught for any man; for thou dost not regard the person of man. Tell us then what you think: is it lawful to give tribute to Caesar or not?"

Israel was part of the Roman Empire at this time and was ruled by the Emperor, or Caesar, in Rome. No one liked to pay taxes to a foreign ruler, but the people had no choice, for the Romans kept large armies in the country to enforce their laws. The Pharisees and other enemies of Jesus also disliked paying tribute to Caesar, but they pretended loyalty to the Roman Empire in order to stay in favor with him. So they put this question to Jesus to trap Him. For if He answered "yes," the people would disown Him. If He answered "no," the Pharisees could denounce Him to the Roman authorities for inciting the people to revolt against the laws of Rome.

Although the question was phrased politely and apparently asked in all innocence, Jesus knew what the Pharisees were trying to do.

"Why do you tempt me, you hypocrites?" He asked them. Then He said, "Show me a coin of the tribute." They handed Him a Roman coin on which was stamped the image and name of the Roman Emperor.

"Whose face and inscription is this?" He asked, holding the coin up for all to see.

"Caesar's," they answered.

Then Jesus said, "Render therefore unto Caesar the things that are Caesar's, and unto God the things that are God's."

THE UNWASHED HANDS

Time and again as He moved among His own people, Jesus found Himself attacked by their religious leaders. He never tried to anger them, but the Pharisees, who regarded themselves as the most religious among the Jews, repeatedly accused Jesus of violating religious rules. Jesus said He had not come to destroy the religion of the Jews, but to carry out the word of God, which the Jews had kept alive among men from the earliest time.

As Jesus became known throughout the land for His miracles and His teachings, the Pharisees frequently sought Him out to denounce Him in public and seek arguments with Him. Some time after the miracle of the feeding of the multitude a group of Pharisees and scribes, those who taught in the Temple, came out from Jerusalem to investigate Jesus.

The first thing they saw was some of the Disciples eating bread without having gone through the traditional ceremony of washing their hands first. The Pharisees seized upon this immediately, for it was a strong tradition among the people that a man must wash his hands before eating; not only for cleanliness, but as a religious ceremony. This was only one of many complicated rules dealing with eating that had come to be regarded as commands of God.

The Pharisees and scribes asked Jesus why His Disciples dared violate the rule of hand washing. Jesus had no objection to washing before eating, but He knew His people had to learn the difference between a traditional rule made by men and the command of God. He had a great message from God, but the leaders could not grasp it, because they were so bound up in petty rules.

Jesus turned upon the Pharisees and called them hypocrites, men who do not really believe what they claim to believe. He recalled a prophecy from the Old Testament that such men would honor the Son of God with their lips, but would not give their hearts to Him.

He told the Pharisees that it was useless for men to pretend to worship, so long as they taught rules made by men as laws of God. He accused them of laying aside the commands of God to follow mere man-made customs and traditions, such as the rules about washing pots and cups only in a certain way.

Then Jesus brought home to them an example of a basic Commandment of their Bible, which they had changed to suit their own ideas of tradition. He pointed out that Moses had commanded, "Honor thy father and thy mother." But, He said, the teaching of the Pharisees permitted a man to escape responsibility to his parents.

Thus the simple act of the Disciples eating with unwashed hands became a lesson. And it was this: that man-made rules, no matter how much they be called religious, must not be mistaken for the commands of God.

THE WIDOW'S MITE

T oward the end of one of his last days in Jerusalem, Jesus retired with his twelve Disciples to the steps of the Women's Court to rest after a long and tiring day. In the distance He could see the Mount of Olives, where He usually retired for the night. But this day He rested first on the stone steps with His faithful followers, before making the journey to the mountain. Across the courtyard from them was the Hall of the Treasury, a large building in front of which were placed thirteen alms boxes. These were for the people to deposit their offerings, to help carry on the work of God.

During the time of the Passover many people flocked to the city. A priest was needed to supervise the payment of the pledges and contributions put into the boxes, and to see that the coins offered were genuine. The alms boxes were labeled so the people would know what their offering was to be used for. As the priest deposited the coins in the box each person could see how much or how little his neighbor had contributed.

As Jesus and the Disciples watched, a poor widow approached to make her offering. She had but two small copper coins to give, which together were worth less than a penny, but they were all she could afford. Being unable to read, and confused at the number of alms boxes, she asked the priest for assistance. He looked at her two small coins, then threw them disdainfully into one of the boxes. At the same time he announced the amount of the gift in a loud voice, so all could hear. The poor woman was embarrassed and ran away into the crowd, which looked at her contemptuously.

Jesus, seeing all of this, and not wanting His Disciples to miss the lesson that had been acted out before their eyes, said to them, "Amen, I say to you, this poor woman has given more than all the rest. For the others have given out of their abundance, whereas she has deprived herself of necessities in giving all that she had."

THE SERMON ON THE MOUNT

S oon after Jesus had chosen His Twelve Disciples, He went with them to Capernaum. There, as usual, a great throng of people had gathered to listen to His teaching. For the news of the miracles of healing He had performed and of the message He brought had gone before Him.

One evening Jesus went out from Capernaum to a mountain not far away, to instruct His Disciples. Many others followed, and thus they became the first to hear the most famous of His sermons—the Sermon on the Mount.

It began with what are called the Beatitudes. Jesus said:

"Blessed are the poor in spirit;
for theirs is the Kingdom of Heaven.

"Blessed are they that mourn;
for they shall be comforted.

"Blessed are the meek;
for they shall inherit the earth.

"Blessed are they which do hunger and thirst after righteousness;
for they shall be filled.

"Blessed are the merciful;
for they shall obtain mercy.

"Blessed are the pure in heart;
for they shall see God.

"Blessed are the peacemakers;
for they shall be called the children of God.

"Blessed are they which are persecuted for righteousness' sake;
for theirs is the Kingdom of Heaven.

"Blessed are ye, when men shall revile you, and persecute you
and shall say all manner of evil against you falsely, for my sake.

"Rejoice, and be exceedingly glad;
for great is your reward in heaven,
for so persecuted they the prophets which were before you."

Then Jesus told those present that He had not come to destroy the old Law, or the prophets, but rather to fulfill them. He enlarged on the old Laws of Moses, giving these examples to make His meaning clear:

"You have heard it said, 'Thou shalt not kill; for whoever kills shall be in danger of judgement.' But I say to you: whoever shall become angry with his brother without cause shall be in danger of judgement.

"You have also heard it said, 'Thou shalt not commit adultery.' But I say to you that whoever looks on a woman with lust is already an adulterer at heart.

"Again you have heard it said, 'Thou shalt not forswear thyself, but shall perform unto the Lord thine oaths.' But I say to you swear not at all, neither by heaven nor earth, by Jerusalem nor by thy head. But let your communication be, yea, yea, nay, nay; for whatsoever is more than those cometh from evil.

"You have heard that it has been said, 'An eye for an eye, and a tooth for a tooth.' And I tell you to not resist this evil. But if anyone strikes thee on the right cheek, then turn to him the left; and if anyone sues thee at law and taketh away thy coat, give him thy cloak also. And whosoever will compel thee to go a mile with him, go with him two. Give to him that asketh of thee, and from him that would borrow from thee turn not away.

"And you have also heard it said, 'Thou shalt love thy neighbor and hate thine enemy.' But I say unto you, love your enemies, bless them that curse you, do good to them that hate you, and pray for those who persecute you, that you may be the children of your father which is in Heaven."

These simple words which Jesus spoke to His Disciples sitting about him, and to the people gathered on the Mountainside, were the guidelines upon which the Christian faith was later to be founded. But at the time the Sermon on the Mount was given by the Lord Jesus, it signalled the beginning of His Gospel, giving an outline of Christian ideals.

ZACCHAEUS

On His last journey to Jerusalem, Jesus stopped off in Jericho, then the second largest city in Israel. It was a beautiful and prosperous city, with many lovely buildings, including an ampitheater, a hippodrome, and even running water brought into the city by pipes. It was also the center of one of the tax-gathering districts, and contained a large treasury building where many tax gatherers, or publicans, were employed.

The chief of these publicans was a rich and powerful man named Zacchaeus, who was hated by the people. He had heard of Jesus, and for some reason he wanted to see this new prophet. Being too short to see above the shoulders of the others, who lined the street where Jesus was to pass by, Zacchaeus climbed a tree so he could catch a glimpse of Him.

Many other persons had also climbed into the trees along the street to see better, but as Jesus came by, Zacchaeus was the only one He paid any attention to. Looking up at the publican, who was not only hated but considered a sinner by the people, Jesus said in a friendly tone of voice, "Zacchaeus, come down quickly, for today I must lodge in your house."

The chief tax gatherer climbed down from his tree and hurried to his home to prepare to receive Jesus. The people following the Lord were much surprised by Jesus' actions and said to one another, "Why does he go to lodge with a sinner?"

They could not know that the look Jesus had given Zacchaeus had transformed the publican. This was apparent when Jesus entered his home with the Disciples. No sooner had they entered than Zacchaeus said to Jesus, "Lord, half of my goods I am going to give to the poor; and if I have wrongly taken from any man, I shall return to him four times as much."

Then Jesus said to the publican, "Today salvation has come to this house; for this man also is a son of Abraham. For the Son of Man came to seek and save that which was lost."

THE TRANSFIGURATION

O ne day Jesus gathered together His Disciples at the foot of the great Mount Hermon and revealed to them that He would arise from death three days later; but the Disciples did not understand. They believed that He would be made a king on earth by the people, for the people had swarmed to Him to hear His words and to seek healing.

A week later Jesus took Peter, John and James up onto Mount Hermon. The Disciples lay down to sleep and Jesus was at prayer when a great change came over His appearance. A great light shone from Him, and His garments became a brilliant white. When the Disciples awoke they saw Jesus thus glorified and talking with Moses and Elijah, two of the greatest of God's Chosen People.

Finally Peter said, "Master, it is good for us to be here. Let us make here three tabernacles, one for you, one for Moses, and one for Elijah."

While he was speaking a cloud came and hovered over them and a voice came out of it, saying, "This is My beloved Son; hear Him." Then the Disciples were alone with Jesus. They were frightened, but He soothed them and reassured them. As they walked down the mountain, Jesus told Peter and James and John not to tell anyone what they had seen until He had risen from the dead.

THE HEALING
OF THE PARALYTIC

During His early ministry in Galilee, word of Jesus' miraculous healing power went before Him. On every side he was beset by crowds of crippled and sick persons who begged Him to heal them. At times Jesus had to seek refuge in the desert, to rest and find a little peace so He might instruct His Disciples.

After one such period in the desert Jesus returned to Capernaum, but entered the town after dark to avoid the multitudes until the following day. But word got around that Jesus was in the town, and the townspeople flocked to His dwelling place to hear Him speak. Even the Pharisees and Scribes came. Of course they never passed up an opportunity to be present when Jesus was teaching, in the hope that they might somehow discredit Him in the eyes of the people.

As Jesus was talking to the many people who had crowded into the house where He was staying that night, four men carrying a paralytic on

a litter came to the door. The crowd was so thick that they could not enter. The house was built around a patio, and the four men, determined that their sick friend should see this miraculous healer, laboriously climbed to the roof. Then they lowered the litter with their friend on it to the floor of the patio, at Jesus' feet.

Seeing this evidence of such strong faith, Jesus said to the man on the litter, "My son, be of good cheer; your sins are forgiven." Jesus believed, as did most of the people of His time, that an incurable sickness such as this man had was a punishment for his sins. The Pharisees heard these words and thought to themselves, "What wicked things this man Jesus speaks. He says He can forgive sins; but only God can do that."

Jesus knew what His enemies were thinking, and He said aloud to them: "Why do you think evil in your hearts? Which is easier to say; 'Thy sins are forgiven thee,' or to say 'Arise, take up thy bed and go away.'?"

No one answered, and then Jesus astounded all those who were present. He looked at them, and said: "Now that you may know that the Son of God has power on earth to forgive sins—," He paused and turned to the paralytic man on the litter, and told him, "Arise, I command thee, take up your bed and go back to your house."

Immediately the man arose from the floor, picked up the litter and went to his home.

The Pharisees were silent. They feared to anger the people who had witnessed this miracle with their own eyes, and who now believed in Jesus even more than before.

THE HEALING
AT BETHESDA'S POOL

Jesus did most of His teaching in the small towns away from the capital city of Jerusalem. But every year He went there to join in the Feast of the Passover.

Each time He went to Jerusalem He upset the religious leaders. These Jewish leaders believed that religion required strict observance of the many rules which had been piling up over the centuries. But Jesus paid no attention to the rules, unless they were commands of God.

During the years of Christ's teachings, as reported in the Bible, the first time He attended the Passover Feast in Jerusalem He drove the money changers out of the Temple.

The second year He went to Jerusalem He sought to go out among the people, not to preach to the crowds, but to help those who needed help. Therefore He went to a pool near the city, which was known as Bethesda's pool. Many sick and crippled people gathered at the pool, because they believed that the waters would heal them.

It was the Sabbath Day when Jesus went out to Bethesda's pool. Near the pool Jesus saw a man lying on a mat. He knew without being

198

told that the man had been crippled for most of his life and was unable to walk.

Jesus asked the man if he wished to be made well. The cripple told Jesus he could not walk and that no one would carry him to the pool. Whenever he tried to crawl there himself, others crowded him out, so that he could not reach the waters which he hoped would cure him.

Jesus said to the man: "Rise, take up your bed and walk."

The man had never heard words like these before, for no one believed he could be cured. But at the sound of His voice he felt new strength. He arose, picked up the mat he had been lying on, and started to walk towards his home.

This was the Sabbath Day, and as we know there were many rules about what could and could not be done on the Sabbath. Someone stopped the man as he left the pool and told him, "It is not lawful to carry your bed on the Sabbath."

The man replied, "He who cured me told me to take up my bed and walk."

They asked him who had told him this. He replied that he did not know who the man was. And of course Jesus had moved away into the crowd, and could not be seen.

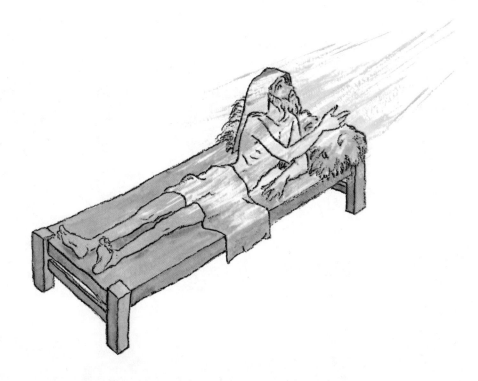

Later, however, Jesus came up to the man in the Temple and said to him, "Behold you have been cured: sin no more lest something worse happen to you."

Then the man recognized Jesus and went to the Jewish leaders and told them that it was Jesus who had cured him. The leaders, already resentful of Jesus, sought to have Him killed for breaking the rules of the Sabbath Day. But He told them that as God worked on all days to do good, so He, as the Son of God, worked the same.

This made the leaders even more angry because Jesus had spoken of God as his father, making himself equal with God.

But Jesus calmly told them that if they did not honor Him as the Son of God they did not honor God, His father.

THE HEALING
OF THE WITHERED HAND

On a Sabbath day while he was in Capernaum, Jesus went into the synagogue to observe the holy day as He usually did. There was in the synagogue a man who had a withered hand. He had come looking for Jesus, hoping that Jesus would cure his hand. The leaders of the Temple were also hoping that Jesus would cure him so they could then accuse Him of breaking the rules of the Sabbath by doing so.

Jesus did not care what the leaders thought of Him; He was only concerned to help those in trouble. He knew that He would be accused of breaking the Sabbath, but He called boldly to the man with the withered hand: "Stand forth."

Then He turned to the people who resented Him and were trying to get Him into trouble with the authorities. He said to them, "Is it lawful to do good on the Sabbath Day or to do evil? To save life or to kill?" No one dared to try to answer His question.

Jesus looked at the people surrounding Him. He was saddened at the hardness of their hearts; that they cared more about challenging Him to break rules, than they cared about seeing a sick man cured.

He asked them, "If a man owns a sheep and it falls into a pit on the Sabbath Day, will he not take hold of it and lift it out? Is not a man worth more than a sheep?"

He turned to the crippled man and told him, "Stretch forth your hand." When the man held out his withered hand, it was restored and had become just as perfect as his other hand.

The Pharisees, who hated Jesus, were furious that their rules had been broken. They went out of the Temple and met together with another group who were supporters of King Herod. Together they planned how they might destroy Jesus.

But Jesus left the town and moved down to the Sea of Galilee. His fame kept growing throughout the country as the word of this and other miracles spread, so that He was followed by great crowds of people who were for Him. And His enemies did not dare to kill Him at this time.

THE HEALING WORDS

One day in Capernaum one of the rulers of the synagogue, a man named Jairus, came to Jesus in a great state of grief. He fell before Jesus and begged him, "My daughter is dying and may even now be dead, but if you come and lay your hand upon her she will live." Thus had the fame of Jesus grown, so that even a leader of the synagogue had complete faith that He could cure his daughter of her terrible sickness.

Jesus rose and followed Jairus, accompanied by some of His Disciples. As they walked along a great throng of people crowded around. Jairus was an important man and they knew of his daughter's illness, and they hoped to see a miracle performed.

In the crowd was a poor woman, who had been very ill for twelve years with a sore that had bled so much that she had grown very weak. She was not able to push through the crowd to speak to Jesus and she could not make herself heard among the throng. But she had great faith

in Jesus and she felt if she could just get close enough to touch the hem of His robe, it would help her. She struggled through the crowd and as Jesus passed she reached out and barely touched the hem of His robe. At that instant she was cured.

Jesus stopped suddenly and turned to His Disciples and asked, "Who touched me?" They were startled at the question because the crowd was pressing on Him from all sides. But Jesus knew that power had gone out from Him to someone who had needed Him and He looked to see who it was. The woman came forward fearing she had done wrong. But Jesus said to her, "Daughter, be of good comfort; your faith has made you well." And the woman remained well from that hour.

Jairus, the father of the dying girl, was naturally impatient for fear Jesus would not arrive in time. And at that very moment a message came that the child had died. But Jesus said to Jairus, "Do not be afraid; only believe, and she will be saved to you."

They moved on to Jairus' house. There they found many friends crying and wailing with grief. Jesus tried to quiet the people. "Weep not," he told them. "She is not dead, but sleeping." Many were bitter and scornful that He seemed to make light of their grief. They knew the child was dead.

Jesus had the people moved out from the room where the child lay. He took with him into the room three Disciples, James, John, and Peter. There lay the dead girl, who was twelve years old. Jesus took her by the hand and told her to rise. She opened her eyes and sat up, completely cured.

As with many of His healing miracles, Jesus told those who knew of this not to talk about it. He often urged those He cured not to tell anybody how the cures had happened. He know that if the people came to think of Him as only a miracle worker, His message for the spirit might be lost in the demands of those who sought only to be cured in the body. The throngs of the merely curious might crowd out those who came to take into their hearts the understanding of God which Jesus brought.

THE HEALING TOUCH

ow everywhere Jesus went His fame had gone before Him. Although communications were slow and poor in those days, somehow the news of His miraculous healings and divine message always managed to precede Him. When Jesus healed the sick or crippled, their cure was usually witnessed by many people, who naturally told their neighbors of what they had seen our Lord do; and so the fame of Jesus spread.

But sometimes He did not want the multitudes to see His wondrous works. He would take the person to be healed aside, with only the Twelve Disciples as witnesses. On two occasions in particular did Jesus use this method to heal sick persons. One was when a dumb man was brought to Him at Decapolis on the east coast of the Sea of Galilee, and the other was when he healed a blind man at the village of Bethsaida, on the Sea of Galilee.

The dumb man could hear nothing, and his speech was incoherent. Jesus led him aside from the people who had brought him to be cured and put His fingers into the man's ears; then He moistened His finger and touched the man's tongue. Lifting His eyes to heaven, Jesus sighed and said to the man, "Be opened." He told the man to say nothing of what had happened. But the man, probably inspired by gratitude, told all he met of the miracle Jesus had performed, increasing His fame even more.

The healing of the blind man was much the same. Coming to Bethsaida from across the Sea of Galilee, Jesus and His Disciples disembarked and were met by a multitude who brought the blind man with them. Jesus led him away from them, moistened his eyes with spittle, and said, "Can you see anything?"

The man looked up and said, "I see men; but they look like trees walking."

Jesus touched his eyes again and the man could see perfectly. Jesus sent him home, saying to him, "Do not go into the village, or tell what has happened here." But this man, like the dumb man, told of the miracle that had cured him. It is not clear why Jesus took these men aside to be healed or told them not to speak of the miracles He had performed. Whatever the reason, the reports of these two cures spread His fame even more.

THE HEALING OF THE TEN LEPERS

During Jesus' last pilgrimage to the Holy City of Jerusalem, He had cause once more to prove His compassion for man through an act of healing. He was traveling with His faithful Disciples from Samaria to Galilee, and as He approached a village to seek shelter one night He was met by ten lepers. These poor afflicted creatures were banned by law from any contact with society, and usually traveled in groups to share their common lot of misery.

These men had heard of Jesus, and they approached to within a respectful distance of the Lord and cried out in unison, "Jesus, Master, have mercy on us."

The distressing condition these poor souls were in—filthy, in rags and covered with sores—and the humility of their plea to Jesus, touched His heart. He turned to them and said, "Go, show yourselves to the priests."

It was the law during those days that any person afflicted with the dreaded leprosy and who claimed to be cured, had to first present his claim to a priest. The priest then examined the person. It was the priest who made the final decision as to whether or not the sick man could again take his place in society as a healthy citizen.

Upon hearing these words, the lepers hastened to obey. This sign of their faith was immediately rewarded, for as they ran to seek out a priest they felt themselves cured. But one of the ten, who was not a Jew but a Samaritan, turned back to Jesus when he saw that he had indeed been cured. Praising God in a loud voice, he threw himself at the feet of Jesus as a sign of his thanks.

Jesus was much moved by this act, and He said to His Disciples, "Were not all of them cured? And where then are the other nine? Has none other than this stranger returned to give glory to God?" Then He said to the Samaritan, "Rise and go; thy faith has saved thee."

THE HEALING OF THE CENTURION'S SERVANT

In the town of Capernaum, where Jesus did much of his teaching and where He returned after many of His trips, there was a company of Roman soldiers, as in all the larger towns of Israel.

The Romans ruled the land as part of the Roman Empire, though they let the Jewish leaders exercise most of the power, under the watchful eye of Rome.

The Romans had grown very broadminded about religious ideas, because they ruled over many lands where there were a great variety of religions. So long as the people paid their taxes and didn't make trouble, the Romans let them practise whatever religion they wished.

The officer in charge of the company in Capernaum was a Roman centurion, a rank we might call captain. This centurion had studied the

Jewish religion and had become very interested in it. He had even built a synagogue where the Jews of Capernaum worshipped. The Jewish leaders respected this Roman, but they could never accept the idea that an outsider could have a truly deep faith in God.

The Roman centurion had heard of Jesus. He had never seen Him or heard Jesus speak, but he had studied His message from God and had come to believe that He was truly a man of God. The centurion had a servant, a young boy of whom he was very fond, and who had fallen sick. When the centurion heard that Jesus was in Capernaum, he asked some of his friends among the leaders of the synagogue to see if Jesus would cure the boy. The elders, as the leaders were called, came to see Jesus and told Him of the centurion. They asked Him if He would come and cure the boy.

Jesus agreed and set out for the centurion's house with the elders. A crowd followed, for they had heard that Jesus might be going to work a miracle. However, before they got to the house, they were met by a messenger from the centurion.

The centurion had been told that Jesus was on His way. Though he was the most powerful man in the city, and could have ordered Jesus to come to him, the centurion sent word that he did not think himself worthy to have such an exalted person as Jesus in his house.

He also explained, through the messenger, that he did not consider himself worthy to come and speak to Jesus. And that was why he had asked the religious leaders to speak, not for himself, but for his sick servant. He urged Jesus not to trouble Himself to come to the servant's side, but asked that Jesus simply speak a word where He was, and he knew his servant would be cured.

Thus the centurion showed his absolute faith in the power of Jesus. The centurion was a man who understood power, for his government gave *him* unquestioned power over all those under him. He explained his faith in Jesus by likening the spiritual power of Jesus under God to his own power as a centurion of Rome, used to having all his earthly commands carried out.

"I also am a man under rule," he said, "and I have soldiers under me, and I say to one, 'Go,' and he goes. And to another, 'Come,' and he comes. And to my servant 'Do this,' and he does it. You too have power to speak and be obeyed. Speak the word and my servant will be cured."

Jesus was impressed by the unquestioning faith of this Roman. Jesus turned to the crowd and said: "In truth I say to you, I have not found so great a faith as this in all Israel."

Then He spoke to the messenger from the centurion, and said: "Go and say to this man, 'As you have believed in me, so shall it be done to you.'"

When the messenger returned to the centurion's house the servant had already been completely cured.

THE RAISING OF LAZARUS

As Jesus traveled about bringing His message to the people, many became believers, and some became His special friends. Among these was a family in Bethany, two sisters and their brother. One of the sisters was Mary. She had been forgiven her sins when she had appeared at the house of Simon, the Pharisee, and anointed the feet of Jesus with ointment, weeping in sorrow over her sins. She had a sister named Martha and a brother, Lazarus. Jesus loved these people and they believed in Him.

Jesus had been driven out of the area in which He lived by those who did not understand Him. He was preparing to move on to another land to preach when the sisters sent Him a message, that Lazarus, their brother, was very ill.

Jesus did not rush back to His friend's side, but told His Disciples that the illness of Lazarus was a part of God's plan for the unfolding of His message.

After two days, however, He told His Disciples they were returning to the part of Judea where they had come from. The Disciples protested that the people there had been ready to stone them. Jesus calmly told them that His friend Lazarus had fallen asleep and He was returning to awaken him. The Disciples did not understand, and said the illness must be passing if Lazarus could sleep. Then Jesus told them plainly that Lazarus was dead. He added that He was glad for their sake that He had not been there to save His friend's life, for if they returned with Him now they would understand His message better.

One of the Disciples, Thomas, spoke up readily and said, "Let us also go that we may die with our Master." He feared the people would kill them, but he was ready to die for Jesus.

They reached Bethany, which was near the capital, Jerusalem; there they found that Lazarus had been dead for four days and was in a tomb, which was a cave closed by a rock. Martha came to meet Jesus and said to Him. "Lord, if you had been here my brother would not have died. And even now I know that whatever you ask from God, God will give you."

Jesus said to her, "Your brother will rise again."

Martha replied that she knew her brother would rise from the dead on the last day of judgment when all the dead would rise, as Christ had preached.

But Jesus said to her, "He who believes in me, though he die, yet shall he live, and whoever lives and believes in me shall never die. Do you believe this?"

Martha replied that she believed that Jesus was the Son of God. She went then to her sister Mary who was surrounded by grieving friends and told her quietly, "The Master is here and is calling for you."

Mary rose and quickly went out with her sister. The friends, thinking she was going to the tomb to mourn, went with her.

When Mary came to Jesus she fell at His feet and said, "Lord, if you had been here, my brother would not have died."

Jesus was deeply moved and said, "Where have you laid him?"

They said, "Come and see."

When Jesus stood at the tomb He wept, and the people gathered there said, "See how He loved Lazarus." Then some said, "Could not He who opened the eyes of the blind man have kept this man from dying?" They were referring to the miracle Jesus had performed earlier.

Then Jesus said, "Take away the stone from the tomb."

Martha protested that Lazarus had been dead four days and his body would be decaying.

Jesus said to her, "Did I not tell you that if you would believe you would see the glory of God?"

So they took away the stone.

And Jesus lifted up His eyes and said, "Father, I thank Thee that Thou hast heard me." When He had said this, He cried with a loud voice, "Lazarus, come out."

The man who had been dead came out of the tomb alive, still wound in the wrappings that they used to bind up the dead. And Jesus said, "Unbind him and let him go."

Those who saw this were astonished, and many came to believe in Jesus and followed Him, but others went to the leaders of the people and told them about this miracle.

These leaders, the chief priests and the Pharisees, who were the ruling group, brought together their council and said, "What are we to do? For this man performs many wondrous things. If we let Him go on thus, everyone will believe in Him and the Romans will no longer accept us as leaders and will destroy our nation."

So they decided that they would find a way to destroy Jesus. But the time had not yet come for the death of Jesus, and He moved on to the land where He had been going when He received the message about Lazarus' illness.

PETER'S CONFESSION OF FAITH

During the last days of His ministry in Galilee, Jesus went off by Himself to be alone with God. After a while he rejoined His Disciples near a place called Caesarea Phillippi. There He walked with them and talked to them at great length. Finally He asked the Twelve Disciples a question.

"What do the people say about the Son of Man, and what am I in their eyes?"

They had many answers to give Him. Each of the Twelve Disciples reported what they had heard the people say about the Lord. Some said the people thought He was John the Baptist. Others mentioned the prophets of olden times, identifying Jesus as Elias or Jeremiah. The people thought, the Disciple said, that Jesus might indeed be one of the

forerunners of the Messiah, but not the Messiah himself.

Jesus listened gravely to these reports and then asked them, "But you, whom do you say that I am? You who are living my life, who have shared my confidences and seen my works; what do you think of me?"

All the other Disciples hesitated to answer Him, but not Simon Peter. "Thou art the Christ, the Son of the living God," Peter said without a second thought.

Jesus was much moved by this confession of Peter's faith, and He addressed His answer to Peter alone as He blessed him and rewarded Him for his faith.

"Blessed are thou, Simon Peter," Jesus said, "because flesh and blood has not revealed this to thee, but My Father who is in heaven. And I say to thee, thou art Peter, and upon this rock I shall build My church, and the gates of hell shall not prevail against it. I will give thee the keys of the kingdom of heaven; and whatsoever you shall bind upon earth shall be bound in heaven, and whatsoever you shall loose upon earth shall be loosed in heaven."

THE MOTHER OF JAMES AND JOHN

As His time of teaching drew toward its end, Jesus told His Disciples what was going to happen to Him in Jerusalem, but they could not believe that He was to be put to death. Of course, they did not want to believe this, because they loved their master. And they could not rid themselves of the idea that Jesus would some day reign as a king on earth. They well knew that He had powers beyond any earthly king. Like most of the Jews, they interpreted the prophecies of the coming of the Saviour of their people, to mean that the Christ, as the prophets called Him, would be a king such as King David.

215

Thus, even as Jesus was preparing to return to Jerusalem for the last time, two of His Disciples, James and John, the sons of Zebedee, approached Him with their mother and knelt before Him. Jesus asked, "What is it you would ask of me?"

The mother replied, "Lord, grant to me that my two sons may be allowed to sit beside your throne, one on the right hand and the other on the left in your kingdom."

"You do not know what you are asking," Jesus replied sorrowfully. "Are you able to drink the cup that I drink?" He was asking if they were able to share the agonies of death which He was soon to face.

"We are able," they said to Him, not really understanding.

"The cup that I drink you will drink," Jesus told them, "but to sit at my right hand or at my left is not mine to grant, but it is for those for whom it has been prepared." He meant that only God, the Father, could make a place in heaven for any man.

When the other Disciples heard of the request of James and John they were angry with the two brothers. But Jesus called them all to Him and said, "You know that those who are supposed to rule over the nations of the world exercise lordship over them, and their great men exercise authority over them. But it shall not be so among you. Whoever would be great among you must first be servant to the rest, and whoever would be first among you must be slave of all. For the Son of Man also came not to be served but to serve, and to give His life as a ransom for many."

THE MINISTRY TO THE MULTITUDES

Though Jesus knew the word of God and was able to teach it to men, He never sought out His listeners. He never invited anyone to come hear Him preach; He never tried to attract attention or to draw a crowd.

When He entered a town, He often spoke in the synagogue, since it was the custom for members of the congregation to speak; but most of His teaching was done wherever he happened to be—in the streets of a town, on the shore of a lake, even out in the country.

These were not formal meetings. Often the occasion for teaching came about because someone came to Jesus to be healed; sometimes He merely responded to a question, often a challenging question by some leader of the community who wanted to know by what authority Jesus was teaching.

But wherever He spoke, all kinds of people were drawn to Him. And for whatever reason they came to hear Him—often probably from idle curiosity because they had heard of His healing miracles—people went away not quite the same as they had been before they heard Jesus' words. This does not mean that everyone who heard Jesus believed in Him. There were some, such as the Pharisees, who were so blinded by pride that they could not learn, and saw in Jesus only a threat to their power. But there were many whose lives were permanently changed by the words of Jesus, and you have read of some of them in this book.

It was often the poor, the outcast, the despised who were best able to understand the truth Jesus taught, for they were not blinded by pride. But the rich and powerful could also be moved by Jesus' words, and it is interesting that some among the ruling Romans came to believe in Him as the Son of God. These were men who had known of many religions and philosophies; they might have been expected to brush aside Jesus, as just another preacher among a people who produced many prophets and teachers.

But whether Roman ruler, poor shepherd, Jewish scholar or any other of the multitudes that heard Jesus, they came to Him; He never needed to call.

THE TRIUMPHAL ENTRY

esus and His Disciples arrived in Bethany on their way to Jerusalem on a Saturday, and there they spent the night. Many people in Jerusalem heard that He was there, and because it was only a short distance from the city, went to see Him. Many also came to see Lazarus, whom Jesus had brought back from the dead. Jesus and His Disciples and Lazarus had supper that night at the home of Simon the Leper, one of those Jesus had healed, and the next day they set out for Jerusalem.

As they left Bethany, a large crowd followed Jesus and His Disciples, and all along the way many more people who had come out from Jerusalem, joined the throng following the Lord. On the road to Jerusalem Jesus suddenly stopped and said to two of His Disciples, "Go into the next village, and at a place where two roads cross you will find an ass tied and a colt with it. Loose them, and bring them to me. And if anyone says to you, 'Why do you do this?' say, 'The Lord has need of them,' and they will let them go."

The two Disciples did as Jesus said, and found the ass and the colt. As they were untying the animals the owner came up and asked them what they were doing. When they told him what Jesus had said, he let them take the ass and colt for Jesus' use.

When the Disciples returned, some of the people with Jesus placed their coats on the colt so it would be more comfortable for Jesus to ride. Others went into the fields to gather flowers, while others cut green palm branches from the trees that lined the road. Then they formed a great procession, and followed Jesus as He rode on the colt toward Jerusalem. The multitudes threw flowers in His path and waved the palm branches in the air and shouted; "Hosanna to the son of David. Blessed is He that cometh in the name of the Lord. Blessed be the kingdom of our Father David, that cometh in the name of the Lord. Hosanna in the highest."

The noise and tumult of the crowd was tremendous as the procession entered the Holy City. The Pharisees who were present were much angered and frightened at this overwhelming reception the people were giving Jesus. They cried out to Him, "Master, silence your Disciples." And Jesus answered them saying, "I tell you, that if they should be silent, these very stones would cry out."

As He rode toward the Temple, people from the city cried out to those following Jesus, "Who is this?" And the multitude answered, "This is Jesus, the prophet of Nazareth in Galilee." And even more joined the procession as Jesus rode toward the Temple. At this the Pharisees became more angry than ever and said, "All our efforts are in vain. Behold the entire world is running after Him." And they realized then that they could not afford to delay any longer in ridding themselves of this prophet from Nazareth.

When Jesus reached the Temple He went in, but did not stay long. It was late and time to retire; so He left the Temple and returned to Bethany with His Disciples and stayed the night there with friends. To-day, throughout Christianity, this day in the Lord's life is celebrated as Palm Sunday.

THE LAST SUPPER

The feast of the Passover is the Jews' annual commemoration of their flight from Egypt, and the meal was then eaten about midnight. In this last year of Jesus' life it fell on a Thursday, and early in the morning the Twelve Disciples asked the Lord, "Where dost thou wish that we go to prepare what is needed to eat for the Passover?"

In answer to them Jesus spoke to Peter and John, saying to them, "Go into the city, and a man carrying a pitcher of water will meet you; follow him, and go into the house where he goes, and say to the head of the house, 'The Master says, "Where is thy guest room that I may eat the Passover with My Disciples?"' And he will show you a large upper room furnished and ready; there prepare the Passover."

All this happened as Jesus said, and the two went out and bought a lamb and roasted it and prepared the vegetables and thin wafers of bread for the supper. Later that afternoon Jesus and the faithful Disciples left Bethany and came into Jerusalem to celebrate the feast set up for them. In the upper room they gathered about the table, sitting on low couches, and had their last meal together.

While they were eating, the Disciples began to argue among themselves as to which of them was superior to the others. Jesus listened with sadness, then rose from His couch and poured a basin full of water. While His Disciples watched in wonder He began to wash their feet, one by one. When He came to Peter, the Disciple protested, saying:

"Lord, dost Thou wash my feet?"

"What I doest thou knowest not," Jesus answered, "but thou shalt know hereafter."

"Thou shalt never wash my feet," Peter protested.

222

"If I wash thee not, then you are none of mine."

Then the Disciple said, "O Lord, wash not only my feet, but my hands and my head, too."

"No, Peter," Jesus answered, "One who has already bathed needs only to wash his feet, and then he is clean. And you are clean, but not all of you." The Lord said this knowing that one among them was a traitor who would soon betray Him to His enemies. Then Jesus spoke to all the Disciples, saying:

"Do you know what I have done to you? You call me Master and Lord, and you speak rightly, for so I am. If, then, I your Lord and Master, have washed your feet, you also ought to wash each other's feet; for I have given you an example that you should do to each other as I have done to you."

Then the Lord became very sad and spoke to them again. "Verily, verily, I say unto you, that one of you who is eating here with Me shall betray Me and give Me up to those who will kill me."

At this all the Disciples looked at one another in horror and each asked in turn, "Lord, is it I?"

"It is one of you that dips his hand into the same dish with Me. The Son of Man indeed goes His way, as it is written, but woe to that man who betrays Him and gives Him up to die. It would be better for that man if he had not been born."

While Jesus was speaking, Peter made a sign across the table to John, who was seated next to the Lord, that he should ask who this traitor was. John whispered to Jesus so that none could hear, "Lord, who is it?"

Jesus answered in a low voice that none but John could hear. "It is the one to whom I will give a piece of bread after I have dipped it in the dish." Then He reached across the table and gave the piece of bread to Judas Iscariot.

Judas got up from the table immediately, though none except John and Jesus knew why, and as he left Jesus said to him, "Do quickly what you have to do."

Before Jesus left the upper room that night, He took a loaf of the unleavened bread and broke off bits and gave them to the remaining Disciples, saying, "Take and eat this, for this is my body which is given for you." Then He took some watered wine and passed the cup to them, saying, "Drink, for this is my blood, which is shed for thee." Then Jesus said, "Do this as often as you would remember me."

Jesus told the Disciples that He was going away and that they could not come with Him, but that they should love one another as He had loved them all. He said He was going to make a place for them in His Father's house, and that when it was ready He would come again and take them with Him. It was very late when they finally left the house where they had eaten their Last Supper together. And Jesus led the eleven Disciples toward the Mount of Olives, seeking a place to rest and pray.

IN THE GARDEN OF GETHSEMANE

I t was still dark when Jesus and the eleven Disciples left the Holy City, where they had just eaten their Last Supper together, and made their way toward the Mount of Olives. On the way He gave them His last instructions, and they were saddened at His words, for they knew He was about to leave them.

Peter was particularly sad. Filled with love for Jesus, he said impulsively, "Lord, why cannot I follow you even now? I will lay down my very life for your sake."

"Amen, I say unto you, Peter," Jesus answered, "that this very night before the cock crows twice, thou shalt deny me thrice."

Peter protested, as did all the others, but Jesus remained silent until they reached a garden at the foot of the mountain. It was a walled grove

of olive trees called Gethsemane. Peter, James and John entered the garden with the Lord, while the others waited outside. The four walked a little way into the orchard. Then Jesus said to the Disciples, "My soul is filled with sorrow; a sorrow that almost kills me. Stay here and watch while I pray."

He went a little further into the trees and threw Himself upon the ground and cried out, "O, my Father, if it be possible, let this cup pass away from me; but thy will, not mine, be done." So great was Jesus' agony that great drops of sweat, like drops of blood, ran off His face to the ground.

During this agony of the Lord the three Disciples fell asleep, and when Jesus returned to them He said to Peter, "Could you not watch one hour with me? Watch and pray, lest you enter into temptation; for the spirit is willing, but the flesh is weak."

He returned to His prayer and cried aloud to heaven, "My Father, if this cup cannot pass away unless I drink it, thy will be done." Once more He found Peter, James and John asleep; so He returned to His prayers without awakening them.

The third time He returned to the three He found them still asleep. Looking down at them He said, "Sleep on, now, and take your rest. Behold, the hour has come when the Son of Man is to be betrayed into the hands of sinners." He heard a sound in the distance which made Him speak to the sleeping Disciples once more. "But no, rise up and let us be going. The traitor is here."

Then they went to where the other eight Disciples were waiting by the gate in the stone wall. And all could hear the clanking armor of the soldiers and see the flickering light of the torches, as the enemies of Jesus approached.

THE BETRAYAL

Judas Iscariot left the house where Jesus and the eleven other faithful Disciples were celebrating the Feast of the Passover and hurried to the home of the High Priest. He had betrayed Jesus for thirty pieces of silver. He meant to collect his reward by leading the enemies of the Lord to His resting place that very night.

When Judas entered the High Priest's house he found a great many people awaiting his arrival. There were the Pharisees and the Scribes, guards from the Temple, and even some Roman soldiers. To make sure there would be no mistake, the High Priest told Judas to give a signal when they came upon Jesus, so the guards would know which man to seize.

"The man whom I shall kiss, that is He; lay hold of Him and do not let Him escape," the traitor said. Then he led them toward the Garden of Gethsemane where he knew Jesus and the other Disciples to be.

When the mob came upon them, Jesus and the Disciples were standing around a small fire, near the gate of the garden wall. The mob stopped a few feet away while Judas, who was in the very front, appeared to be looking for someone in the group standing near the fire. Then he ran forward and embraced Jesus.

"Judas," Jesus said, "Do you betray the Son of Man with a kiss?"

As the Temple guards ran forward to seize Him, Jesus advanced to meet them.

"Whom do you seek?" He asked them.

"Jesus of Nazareth," they answered.

"I am He."

At these words the guards fell to the ground in fear, for they had heard of the miraculous powers of Jesus and were afraid He might use these powers to seek vengeance upon them. But when they saw that the Lord was standing quite motionless before them, they regained their courage and rose to their feet once more.

Again Jesus asked: "Whom do you seek?"

"Jesus of Nazareth," said the guards.

Pointing to His Disciples, Jesus said: "I told you that I am He. If it is I that you seek, let these men who are with me go their way."

The betrayal of Jesus by Judas was now complete. But the traitor did not live long enough to enjoy his thirty pieces of silver. When Jesus was crucified, Judas was so overcome with remorse for what he had done, that he went to the Temple. He threw the pieces of silver in the faces of the priests and then went out and hanged himself.

THE HEALING OF THE GUARD'S EAR

hen the Temple guards of the High Priest moved to seize Jesus in the Garden of Gethsemane, after Judas had betrayed Him, the impetuous Apostle, Peter, made one last effort to save the Lord. Drawing his sword he rushed at the enemies of Jesus and cut off the right ear of one of them.

But Jesus stopped Peter, saying to him, "Put up thy sword; the cup which my Father has given me, shall I not drink it? Do you not know that

I could call upon my Father, and he would send to me armies upon armies of angels?"

Then turning to the crowd He said, "Let me do this." He touched the wounded man's ear and it was healed as new.

Once again He addressed the mob before they seized and bound Him. "As against a robber you have come out, with swords and clubs to seize me. I was teaching daily in the Temple, where you could have laid hands upon me; but it must be that the writings of the prophets have their fulfillment; and this is your hour."

When the Disciples saw that Jesus would not let them fight for Him, they did not know what to do. In this sudden state of confusion, they ran away, leaving the Lord alone with his enemies. The Temple guards then seized and bound Jesus and led Him away to the home of the High Priest.

THE TRIAL BEFORE PONTIUS PILATE

After Jesus had been betrayed and captured, He was taken to the home of the High Priest, where the priests and the scribes all voted that Jesus should be put to death. But the land was ruled by the Romans, and no man could be put to death without the consent of the Roman governor. So the enemies of the Lord took Him, still bound, to the palace of the governor, a man named Pontius Pilate.

Pilate took Jesus into an inner room of the court to question Him, then returned to the mob and said, "I find no evil in this man." But the enemies of Jesus persisted, so Pilate, not wanting to be troubled with the case, sent Jesus and His accusers to the court of King Herod. Herod ruled Galilee from whence Jesus came, and so could judge the case. But Herod,

too, could find no evil in Jesus, and sent Him back to Pilate.

So Pilate, much against his will, was forced to decide for or against Jesus. And as Jesus was standing bound before him, the Roman governor received a message from his wife saying, "Do nothing against that good man; for in this night I have suffered many things in a dream on account of him."

Pilate said to the priests and the scribes, "You have brought this man to me as one who is leading the people into evil; and I have found no evil in Him, nor has Herod. Now I will order that He be beaten with rods and set free, for you know that it is the custom to set one prisoner free at the time of the Feast."

This was, indeed, the custom, but the priests went among the people and urged them to ask that Barabbas, a thief and murderer, be set free instead. The people set up a great clamor and cried for Barabbas to be set free. Then Pilate said, "What, then, shall I do with this man Jesus?"

"Crucify Him," the crowd yelled. "Let Him die on the cross."

Pilate did not wish to kill Jesus, and to show how he felt, he sent for a basin of water. Washing his hands in the water he said to the people, "my hands are clean of the blood of this good man."

And the mob cried out, " Crucify Him! Send Him to the cross!"

Pilate tried once more to save the Lord. He had his soldiers beat Jesus and dress Him in a purple robe and set a crown of thorns upon His head, hoping to gain pity for Jesus. "Hail, King of the Jews," the soldiers mocked. But the crowd would not be moved, and once again cried out, "Crucify Him! Send Him to the cross!"

At last Pilate yielded to the people, and commanded that Jesus be put to death on the cross.

THE CRUCIFIXION

I t was the custom in the land that as soon as a man was condemned to death, he must be executed. So as soon as Pontius Pilate signed Jesus' death sentence, He was led to the place of execution. This was a hill outside Jerusalem called Golgotha, or Calvary in the Roman language. It meant "the skull place."

Carrying the cross on which He was to die, Jesus started toward Calvary, guarded by a detachment of Roman soldiers and followed by a large multitude of people. Along the way Jesus stopped in front of a group of women who knew Him and who were weeping because of what was happening to Him. "Daughters of Jerusalem, "He said to them, "do not weep for me, but for yourselves and for your children. For the days are coming when they shall count those happy who have no little ones to be slain; when they shall wish that the mountains might fall on them, and the hills might cover them and hide them from their enemies."

When the procession reached the appointed place, Jesus was nailed to a cross between two criminals who were being cruicified with Him. After they had finished their terrible task, the soldiers guarding Jesus knelt before the cross on which He was dying and cast dice for His robe and other belongings.

Jesus' mother and many who loved Him were there, weeping and mourning the passing of their beloved Saviour. But His enemies were there too and they mocked Him, saying, "If you are the Son of God, come down from the cross." Jesus was silent, then He uttered a short prayer:

"Father, forgive them, for they know not what they do."

A little later, one of the criminals being crucified with Jesus cried out against Him saying, "Art thou not the Christ? Save thyself, then, and us with thee." But the other criminal rebuked him saying, "Dost not even thou fear God, when you are suffering the same fate as this man? Our suffering is the penalty of our crimes; but this man, what evil has He done?" Then he spoke to Jesus saying, "Lord, remember me when thou comest into thy kingdom." And Jesus answered him, as they were both hanging from their crosses, saying:

"Amen, I say to thee, this day thou shalt be with me in paradise."

The next time the Lord spoke during His ordeal on the cross was When He saw His mother, Mary, standing with His Disciple John. He raised His head and said to His mother:

"Behold thy son." And to John He said, "Behold thy mother."

About three o'clock in the afternoon Jesus spoke again, so abruptly that all present were startled at His voice.

"My God, My God! Why hast thou forsaken me?"

The fifth time Jesus spoke from the cross He said:

"I thirst."

Hearing this, one of the more compassionate Roman soldiers on guard raised a sponge dipped in thin wine to the Lord's lips.

Then Jesus bowed His head as if to sleep, but raised it to speak once more as the spirit left Him.

"Father, into thy hands I commend my spirit."

As Jesus hung on His cross, one of the Roman soldiers pierced His side with his spear to be sure He was dead. When His friends saw that Jesus was indeed dead, they went into Jerusalem and asked Pilate if they might take His body, and the Roman governor agreed. Jesus' body was taken from the cross and anointed. Then they wrapped it in linens and placed the body in a cave near Calvary.

THE WOMEN AT THE TOMB

Early Monday morning, three days after His death upon the cross, some women came to Jesus' tomb bearing fragrant ointments and spices to place in the linen wrappings about the Lord's body. Mary Magdelene led the way, and as they walked the women asked one another, "Who will roll away the great stone they have placed at the mouth of the cave?" The High Priest had asked that the tomb be sealed and guarded by soldiers, because he feared the Disciples and friends of Jesus might try to steal His body, and say he had risen from the dead.

When Mary Magdelene approached the tomb she saw the rock had been rolled away and the soldiers had departed. They did not know that before they had come to the tomb, Jesus had emerged from the cave without the soldiers on guard seeing Him. Then an angel had come down from heaven and sat on the stone in front of the tomb, and a great light shone forth from his face. The Roman soldiers were frightened by what they saw and ran away.

But when Mary Magdalene and the other women arrived at the tomb they saw only that the stone had been rolled away from the door. Mary Magdalene immediately ran to tell the Disciples, and the other women entered the tomb. They saw within two angels sitting where the body of the Lord had been.

"Do not be afraid," one of them said. "You are looking for Jesus of Nazareth, who was crucified. He is not here. He is risen, as He said that He would rise from the dead. Come, see the place where the Lord lay; and then go and tell His Disciples, and tell Peter too, that Jesus will go before you into Galilee, and you shall see Him there."

The women left, afraid but joyful, to tell the Disciples what the angels had said. Mary Magdalene, in the meantime, had found Peter and John and told them the tomb was empty. They came to see for themselves, and then they too left. When Mary Magdalene returned alone to the place where Jesus had been buried she was weeping; she entered the tomb and she saw the two angels, one at the foot and one at the head of where Jesus' body had been.

"Woman, why do you weep?" one of them asked.

"Because they have taken away my Lord and I do not know where they have laid Him," she answered. Then she turned and saw Jesus standing near her, but she did not recognize Him. "Sir," she said, "if you have carried Him out of this place, tell me where you have laid Him and I will take Him away."

Then Jesus said to her, "Mary." At the sound of her name she knew it was Jesus standing there, no longer dead, but living. She threw herself to the ground and cried, "My master," and reached to embrace the feet of the Lord.

But Jesus said to her, "Touch me not, for I am not yet ascended to my Father. But go to my brothers and say to them, I ascend to my Father and to your Father, to my God, and to your God."

And still weeping, Mary Magdalene, the first to see Jesus after He had risen from the dead, hastened to tell the Disciples what she had seen and what Jesus had said to her.

JESUS APPEARS TO THE WOMEN

The other women who had gone to the tomb with Mary Magdalene left that holy place after the angel had spoken to them and hastened to Jerusalem to tell the Disciples what they had seen and heard. They did not know that Mary had returned to the cave where Jesus had been buried and had been the first to see the Lord after His Resurrection.

These good women knew only that their Master was no longer in the tomb; that the angel had said that Jesus had risen; and that He would see the Disciples again. They walked toward Jerusalem along the road which only two days before Jesus had traveled to Calvary and the Cross.

When they entered the gates of the city they stopped for a moment to discuss where they should go to look for the Disciples to tell them the news of Jesus' Resurrection. As they were talking in the street a man appeared before them. It was the Lord.

"All hail," He said to them.

They recognized Jesus and were afraid, for they did not understand this appearance, and they fell to the ground in front of the Lord. Jesus took pity on the frightened women and tried to give them comfort and to instruct them.

"Be not afraid," He said, "but find my brothers, and tell them to go into Galilee, and they shall see me there." And then He vanished from their sight. This was the second time they had been told to tell the Disciples that they would see the Lord in Galilee, and they hurried to obey Jesus' command.

EMMAUS

On the day of Jesus' Resurrection, two pilgrims left Jerusalem after visiting the Holy City for several days, for the Feast of the Passover. They were from the village of Emmaus, about seven miles from Jerusalem, and were followers of Jesus. As they walked sadly along the road that morning toward their home, they discussed the events of the past few days. Suddenly they noticed a stranger walking along beside them, and stopped in surprise.

The stranger was Jesus, but His two followers from Emmaus did not know this. The Lord asked them, "What were you saying to one another that seems to have made you so sad?"

One of the men, whose name was Cleopas, said, "Are you even a stranger in Jerusalem, and have not heard of what things have taken place there the past few days?"

"What things?" Jesus asked.

240

"The things regarding Jesus of Nazareth," Cleopas answered, "He who was a prophet mighty in His acts and words before God and the people; and how the chief priests and the rulers caused Him to be condemned and crucified. We had hoped that He was to be the promised one who was to save Israel. It is now three days since all this happened. And this morning, some women of our company who were early at His tomb, found that it was empty except for a vision of angels. The angels told them that Jesus was alive. Then some of us went to the tomb and saw it was as the women had said, but they did not see Him."

"O foolish men, and slow of heart to believe what the prophets have said," Jesus answered, "was it not needful for the Christ to suffer these things, and then enter in His glory?" Then the Lord began to explain to them all the meanings of the prophecies concerning Him, beginning with those of Moses and on down through the Scriptures. As He talked they came to the place where the men from Emmaus had to turn off the road for their home. Jesus made as if to continue on His way, but the two men insisted that He stay the night with them. "Abide with us," they said, "for it is now almost evening, and the day is at its close.

Jesus went with them into their house, and as they sat down for supper He took the bread and blessed it and then broke it and gave it to them. At that moment they recognized the Lord, for they had often seen Him perform this ritual at meals. But as they looked at Him, He disappeared from their sight."

"Were not our hearts burning within us while He talked to us on the road?" they said to one another, "while He opened to us the word of the Scriptures." Then they hastened to retrace their steps to Jerusalem to tell the Disciples of what they had seen.

When they reached the Holy City, well after dark, they found ten of the Disciples in the upper room where they had celebrated the Last Supper with Jesus. Thomas was not there. But when they told the ten of what had happened on the road to Emmaus and in their house, there was doubt among the Disciples, until Jesus suddenly appeared to them and spoke to them—so that all would believe that He was indeed alive.

JESUS APPEARS ON THE SHORE

week or so after the Resurrection, the eleven Disciples left Jerusalem for Galilee, for Jesus had promised to see them there. They camped on the shore of the Lake of Tiberias as they waited for Jesus to show Himself to them. One night, when they were without food, seven of the Disciples, led by Peter, took a boat and some nets out into the lake to fish.

They were having no luck, and as daylight broke they decided to give it up, when a man hailed them from the shore. It was Jesus, but they did not recognize Him.

"My children," Jesus called to them, "do you have any fish?"

"No!"

"Cast your net on the other side of the boat, and you will find some," Jesus called back.

They did, and the net was filled with fish. John looked at the stranger on the shore, and recognized Jesus. "It is the Lord," he said to Peter. Peter jumped into the water and swam to where Jesus stood on the shore, while the others rowed the boat to land.

"Bring some of the fish that you have caught," Jesus said to them. They did, and found they had caught one hundred and fifty three fish in all. When they had cooked some, Jesus said, "Come now and eat!" He broke bread and gave it to them with the fish. After they had breakfasted, He turned to Peter, who had denied Him three times after He had been betrayed in the olive grove outside Jerusalem:

"Simon Peter, son of Jonas," Jesus said to Peter, "lovest thou me?"

"Yes Lord, Thou knowest that I love Thee."

"Feed my lambs," Jesus said to him.

After a while Jesus spoke to Peter again, "Simon Peter, son of Jonas, dost thou love me?"

Peter answered Jesus as before.

"Tend my sheep," Jesus said.

Then for the third time Jesus asked Peter the same question.

This troubled Peter, and he said, "Lord, Thou knowest all things; Thou knowest that I love Thee."

Once again Jesus said, "Tend my sheep." And in this way the Lord showed that He had regained His faith in Peter and that Peter would found His church.

DOUBTING THOMAS

The Disciple Thomas was not present that first Sunday when Jesus appeared to the other Disciples and to the two men from Emmaus in the upper room where Jesus had eaten the Last Supper. When the others told Thomas they had seen the Lord, Thomas said to them, "I will not believe that He has risen unless I can see upon His hands the marks of the nails on the cross. I must see them with my own eyes, and put my hand into the wound in His side, before I will believe."

The following Sunday the Disciples again gathered in the upper room of the house in Jerusalem, and this time Thomas was with them. The door leading to the room was shut, but suddenly the Disciples saw Jesus standing in the middle of the room.

"Peace be with you," He said to them.

Then addressing Himself to Thomas, Jesus said to the doubting Disciple; "Thomas, come here, and touch my hands with your finger, and put your hand into my side; and no longer refuse to believe that I am living, but have faith in me!"

Thomas approached the Lord as all watched, and reached out his hand, but then his doubts left him and he cried out in humble supplication, "My Lord and my God!"

Jesus answered His Disciple saying, "Because you have seen me, you have believed; blessed are they that have not seen, and yet have believed."

THE ASCENSION

The eleven Disciples remained in Galilee for two or three weeks, before they returned to Jerusalem. They were certain they would see Jesus again, but they did not know where or when. They were gathered around the table, in the upper room of the house in Jerusalem, when the Lord appeared before them for the last time.

He sat with them at the table and made them promise not to leave the city until God should send down upon them His spirit.

"John," He told them, "baptised with water, but you shall be baptised with the Holy Spirit in a few days."

The Disciples listened carefully to His words, for some of them had the feeling that this really was the last time they would see their Master. But some asked, "Lord, will you at this time restore the kingdom of Israel?"

"It is not for you to know the time the Father has fixed," He said, "but when the power of the Holy Spirit comes down upon you, you shall speak in my name in Jerusalem and in all of Judea and Samaria and even the ends of the earth."

Then He led His Disciples out of Jerusalem towards Bethany and stopped at the top of the Mount of Olives. Jesus lifted His hands to bless them and then slowly He began to rise up in the air, until a cloud hid Him from the sight of the Disciples.

While they were still witnessing His Ascension into Heaven, two

angels appeared before the Disciples, and said to them: "O ye men of Galilee, why do you stand looking up into Heaven? This Jesus who has been taken from you shall come again from Heaven to earth, as you have seen Him go up from earth to Heaven."

SELECTED PSALMS

FOR

ALL FAITHS

Answer me when I call, O God
of my right!
Thou hast given me room when
I was in distress.
Be gracious to me, and hear my
prayer.

O men, how long shall my honor
suffer shame?
How long will you love vain
words, and seek after lies?
Selah
But know that the LORD has set
apart the godly for him-
self;
the LORD hears when I call to
him.

Be angry, but sin not;
commune with your own hearts
on your beds, and be silent.
Selah
Offer right sacrifices,
and put your trust in the LORD.

There are many who say, "O that
we might see some good!
Lift up the light of thy counte-
nance upon us, O LORD!"
Thou hast put more joy in my
heart
than they have when their grain
and wine abound.

In peace I will both lie down and
sleep;
for thou alone, O LORD, makest
me dwell in safety.

psalm 6

O LORD, rebuke me not in thy
anger,
nor chasten me in thy wrath.
Be gracious to me, O LORD, for I
am languishing;
O LORD, heal me, for my bones
are troubled.
My soul also is sorely troubled.
But thou, O LORD—how long?

Turn, O LORD, save my life;
deliver me for the sake of thy
steadfast love.
For in death there is no remem-
brance of thee;
in Sheol who can give thee
praise?

I am weary with my moaning;
every night I flood my bed with
tears;

I drench my couch with my
weeping.
My eye wastes away because of
grief,
it grows weak because of all my
foes.

Depart from me, all you workers of
evil;
for the LORD has heard the sound
of my weeping.
The LORD has heard my supplication;
the LORD accepts my prayer.

All my enemies shall be ashamed
and sorely troubled;
they shall turn back, and be put
to shame in a moment.

psalm 9

I will give thanks to the LORD
with my whole heart;
I will tell of all thy wonderful
deeds.
I will be glad and exult in thee,
I will sing praise to thy name, O
Most High.

When my enemies turned back,
they stumbled and perished before thee.

For thou hast maintained my just
cause;
thou hast sat on the throne giving righteous judgment.

Thou hast rebuked the nations,
thou hast destroyed the
wicked;
thou hast blotted out their name
for ever and ever.
The enemy have vanished in everlasting ruins;
their cities thou hast rooted out;
the very memory of them has perished.
But the LORD sits enthroned for
ever,
he has established his throne for
judgment;
and he judges the world with righteousness,
he judges the peoples with
equity.

The LORD is a stronghold for the
oppressed,
a stronghold in times of trouble.
And those who know thy name put
their trust in thee,
for thou, O LORD, hast not forsaken those who seek thee.

Sing praises to the LORD, who
dwells in Zion!
Tell among the peoples his
deeds!

For he who avenges blood is mind-
ful of them;
he does not forget the cry of the
afflicted.

Be gracious to me, O Lord!
Behold what I suffer from those
who hate me,
O thou who liftest me up from
the gates of death,
that I may recount all thy praises,
that in the gates of the daughter
of Zion
I may rejoice in thy deliverance.

The nations have sunk in the pit
which they made;
in the net which they hid has
their own foot been caught.
The Lord has made himself known,
he has executed judgment;
the wicked are snared in the
work of their own hands.
Higgaion. Selah

The wicked shall depart to Sheol,
all the nations that forget God.

For the needy shall not always be
forgotten,
and the hope of the poor shall
not perish for ever.

Arise, O Lord! Let not man prevail;
let the nations be judged before
thee!

Put them in fear, O Lord!
Let the nations know that they
are but men! *Selah*

psalm 13

How long, O Lord? Wilt
thou forget me for ever?
How long wilt thou hide thy face
from me?
How long must I bear pain in my
soul,
and have sorrow in my heart all
the day?
How long shall my enemy be exalted over me?

Consider and answer me, O Lord
my God;
lighten my eyes, lest I sleep the
sleep of death;
lest my enemy say, "I have pre-
vailed over him";
lest my foes rejoice because I am
shaken.

But I have trusted in thy steadfast
love;
my heart shall rejoice in thy salvation.
I will sing to the Lord,
because he has dealt bountifully
with me.

psalm 23

The LORD is my shepherd, I
  shall not want;
   he makes me lie down in green
   pastures.
He leads me beside still waters;
  he restores my soul.
He leads me in paths of righteousness
   for his name's sake.

Even though I walk through the
   valley of the shadow of death,
  I fear no evil;
for thou art with me;
  thy rod and thy staff,
  they comfort me.

Thou preparest a table before me
  in the presence of my enemies;
thou anointest my head with oil,
  my cup overflows.
Surely goodness and mercy shall
  follow me
  all the days of my life;
and I shall dwell in the house of
  the LORD
  for ever.

psalm 27

The LORD is my light and my
  salvation;
  whom shall I fear?
The LORD is the stronghold of my
  life;

of whom shall I be afraid?

When evildoers assail me,
  uttering slanders against me,
my adversaries and foes,
  they shall stumble and fall.

Though a host encamp against me,
  my heart shall not fear;
though war arise against me,
  yet I will be confident.

One thing have I asked of the
  LORD,
  that will I seek after;
that I may dwell in the house of
  the LORD
  all the days of my life,
to behold the beauty of the LORD,
  and to inquire in his temple.

For he will hide me in his shelter
  in the day of trouble,
he will conceal me under the cover
  of his tent,
  he will set me high upon a rock.

And now my head shall be lifted up
  above my enemies round about
  me;
and I will offer in his tent
  sacrifices with shouts of joy;
I will sing and make melody to the
  LORD.

Hear, O LORD, when I cry aloud,

be gracious to me and answer me!
Thou hast said, "Seek ye my face."
  My heart says to thee,
"Thy face, LORD, do I seek."
  Hide not thy face from me.

Turn not thy servant away in anger,
  thou who hast been my help.
Cast me not off, forsake me not,
  O God of my salvation!
For my father and my mother have
    forsaken me,
  but the LORD will take me up.

Teach me thy way, O LORD;
  and lead me on a level path
  because of my enemies.
Give me not up to the will of my
    adversaries;
  for false witnesses have risen
    against me,
  and they breathe out violence.

I believe that I shall see the good-
    ness of the LORD
  in the land of the living!
Wait for the LORD;
  be strong, and let your heart take
    courage;
  yea, wait for the LORD!

psalm 101

I will sing of loyalty and of
    justice;
  to thee, O LORD, I will sing.
I will give heed to the way that is

blameless.
  Oh when wilt thou come to me?

I will walk with integrity of heart
    within my house;
I will not set before my eyes
  anything that is base.

I hate the work of those who fall
    away;
  it shall not cleave to me.
Perverseness of heart shall be far
    from me;
  I will know nothing of evil.

Him who slanders his neighbor
    secretly
  I will destroy.
The man of haughty looks and arro-
    gant heart
  I will not endure.

I will look with favor on the faith-
    ful in the land,
  that they may dwell with me;
he who walks in the way that is
    blameless
  shall minister to me.

No man who practices deceit
  shall dwell in my house;
no man who utters lies
  shall continue in my presence

Morning by morning I will destroy
  all the wicked in the land,
cutting off all the evildoers
  from the city of the LORD.

254

This selection of inspirational verse is from The Book of Psalms.